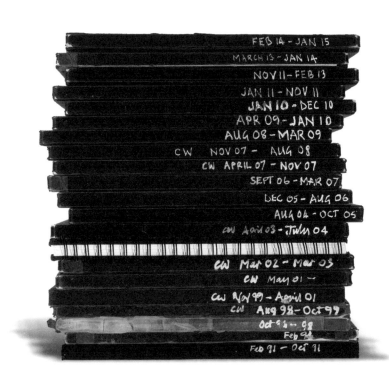

Royal Academy of Arts

THE SKETCHBOOKS OF
CHRIS WILKINSON

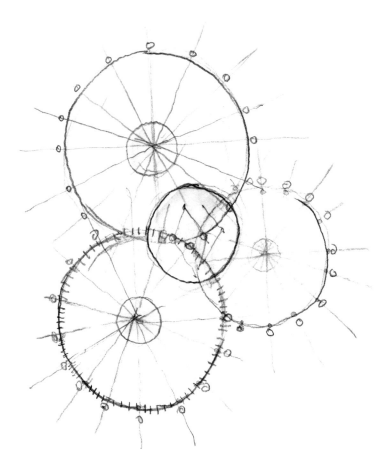

Contents

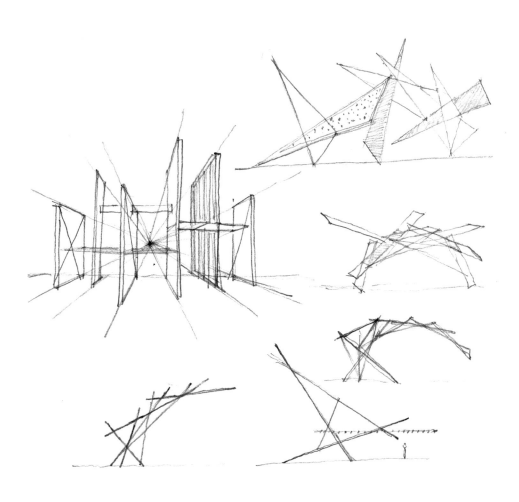

Chris Wilkinson OBE RA is one of the many artists and architects whom I have got to know since becoming Secretary and Chief Executive of the Royal Academy. He is someone who is very obviously committed to the Academy and its public role in representing the work of its members. In recent years Chris has given up much time to serve on Council and, more especially, to chair the Client Committee, which has been responsible for the development of our plans for the future.

Through knowing Chris at the Academy, I have also become a great admirer of his work and his practice. Some of it I knew even before I arrived: Magna in Rotherham, the highly inventive science centre in a disused industrial building that won the Stirling Prize for architecture in 2001; the Gateshead Millennium Bridge – curving across the River Tyne to connect Newcastle to its long-standing urban rival to the south – which won the Stirling Prize the following year; and the elegant twisting footbridge that connects the Royal Opera House in London to the Royal Ballet School across the street. I remember seeing the Stratford Market Depot, one of the early projects on the then new Jubilee line, when I was a judge on the Building of the Year Award some time in the mid-1990s.

More recently, I was taken round the amazing Wilkinson Eyre project in Singapore: Gardens by the Bay, which consists of great bubble domes of exotic botanical specimens celebrating biodiversity in an equatorial city. I am very familiar with Arts Two, the project Chris and his firm completed recently on the campus of Queen Mary, University of London, which includes a ceramic façade of books by Jacqueline

Poncelet – an example of his willingness to collaborate with artists. For the Summer Exhibition in 2012, Chris designed a very beautiful, extremely simple, geometric installation for the Annenberg Courtyard that consisted of a series of frames converting from landscape to portrait.

What I didn't know – but it doesn't at all surprise me – is the extent to which Chris thinks about the process of designing new building projects by way of drawing in a sketchbook that he carries with him. I love the way he describes the process of drawing, in the introduction to this book, as a system of facilitation for the process of thinking, working out his ideas on paper. He does this not with any conscious aesthetic intent, but the results are frequently aesthetically pleasing precisely because they are pure expressions of design thinking.

What one sees in this book are the different ways in which Chris uses drawings: the outline doodle; the slightly more worked-out sketch; the ground plan showing the use of space; the more finished watercolour; the presentation drawing done to seduce a client; the depiction of a particular detail which is worrying him; the drawing which looks as if it has been done for pure pleasure. They are infinitely various and demonstrate clearly the ways in which he uses drawing as a visual language, something that is sadly now rare.

Charles Saumarez Smith CBE
Secretary and Chief Executive,
Royal Academy of Arts

Drawing what I think

CHRIS WILKINSON

When an artist draws from life, he draws what he sees and interprets it in his own way, so that the observer perceives the subject through the artist's eyes. When an architect is designing, he draws what he is thinking and the drawings are part of the creative process. They provide information about the design that can be translated into built form. The artist's work can be an end in itself and can be admired as a thing of beauty, but the architect's sketch might be the germ of an idea, perhaps the start of a great building.

The creative design process is complex and hard to define, but when ideas are generated the simplest way of communicating them is by drawing. For me, the design process starts with getting to know the brief and analysing the site context. This is followed by a series of sketches in which I explore ideas. I start by drawing what I know and then develop ideas as they come through. These early drawings may lead somewhere or they may trigger a thought process for discussion with other members of the design team. Since architecture is a collaborative activity, drawing becomes the language of communication and a few well-chosen lines often convey thoughts better than words can.

Of course, the language of drawing requires a vocabulary. For an architect this involves plans, sections, elevations, perspectives and axonometric projections. In the past, most architects started with plans and sections to develop spatial layouts, and then moved into 3D to work up the form; however, with complex shapes you have to explore in 3D from the start. I tend to start with rough perspective and axonometric sketches because that's how I think. Drawings explain concepts, spatial arrangements,

circulation, structure and details. The process starts with ideas and concepts, continues with layouts and leads on to construction details.

I work on several projects at a time, each in a different stage of development, and so my sketchbooks cover the whole design process. They often jump from early competition sketches on one project to structural details on another. I don't see them as artwork, but as part of a workmanlike design process of turning ideas into buildings. They tell only part of the story, though it is an important part. In addition to my sketchbooks, I carry a notebook for recording meetings and discussions, which I like to keep separate. There are also many drawings made around the table during design discussions, often on 10-inch rolls of detail paper, following an old architectural tradition involving overlays onto a base drawing.

Today, of course, most drawings in the office are made on a computer and there is less emphasis on drawing by hand, but I think that drawings produced manually are still an important part of the process. In my office, we work in 3D from the start yet we still find it necessary to print out drawings and pin them up for discussion. Since I don't use a computer for drawing, my sketchbooks set me apart from the working teams: the discussions we have are more conceptual and vitally important. I produce sketches at the start of projects or competitions, when we are exploring ideas that can be tested in Rhino Grasshopper, a 3D-drawing programme. I also continue to develop drawings informed by 3D models to help progress the design process. We are always looking for an innovative approach and are keen to explore new ideas at every stage.

Some of my sketchbook drawings are made in design meetings but many are carried out during quiet, contemplative moments when I am able to concentrate on a particular design problem. This might be in the office, at home or even when I'm travelling. Time to think is a good time to draw. I carry all the projects I'm working on around in my head, so there are always problems that need solving. I find concerts particularly fruitful opportunities: my mind wanders freely, and ideas seem to emerge out of the blue. Then I can't wait to get back to my sketchbook and test them out.

In the early stages of a design, one has to assimilate huge amounts of information about the brief, the client and the site context. At the start, it seems impossible to tie all of this together in any tangible way, but gradually things start to make sense and ideas emerge that could lead to a solution. These have to be thoroughly tested and yet somehow, out of the complexity of the problem, a clear concept appears, like magic. Just like the rabbit that jumps out of the hat, a design solution materialises that makes sense of all the data one has been struggling with.

It's a process that I love, although it brings with it much mental turmoil and anxiety. For me, there is nothing better than having a new project to sort out, but it doesn't end there: many projects take years to complete and one has to keep up the enthusiasm throughout the whole process. For instance, I have included here an early concept sketch for the King's Cross Gasholders competition dated 29 February 2002 and a later drawing from 2014, in which the same ideas had been developed in the run up to construction in 2015. The delay was related to a phasing programme for the whole of the King's Cross Redevelopment site, of which the Gasholders are only a small part. In other instances, major projects take a long time to progress. The Crown Hotel, Sydney, for example, was first talked about in December 2012, won in competition in August 2013 and is expected to be completed in 2019. My sketchbooks provide an invaluable record of ideas worked through and concepts secured, and they take you back to the inspirational moment when they were drawn – I find this a great help, given the often lengthy timescales of architectural processes.

Alongside architectural projects, I have included drawings of other ideas I have been working on and sketches of places I have visited. The ironmongery concept came about as a request from Edwin Heathcote to produce an ironmongery design for one of our buildings, but that has still to be realised. The triangular table for the Maggie's Centre in Oxford, which I worked on with my colleagues Sebastien Ricard and Andrew Walsh, has been constructed and is located in the central kitchen area. I have tried to design my ideal chair, but the perfect solution has so far eluded me. I also enjoy drawing what I see, so my sketchbooks contain illustrations of places I visit. I love drawing buildings and urban spaces, and my travels are often interrupted by the need to stop and put pen to paper.

Looking through the sketchbooks, which cover the twenty years from 1994 to 2014, I am conscious of the variety of drawing styles and techniques they contain; this is not intentional but it is related to the materials I have available and the mood I am in at the time. I have experimented with different media but my preference is for the 0.9 mm Pentel P209 retractable

pencil; at times I also use a black 0.4 mm Artline 200 pen. More recently I have become interested in using watercolour and find that a splash of pigment can enliven a drawing, adding emphasis where it seems appropriate and reducing the need for more lines. It is a difficult medium to control and the uneven blobs of intensity settle in their own way, adding character and imperfection. This challenges my natural desire to tidy things up and create order, but it is essential to keep away from the chocolate-box image.

Some drawings take time to prepare and the process seems protracted, while others are almost instantaneous. I suspect the time they require is related to the clarity of my thinking at that moment, and the complexity of the problem. Often the first quick sketches, when they are free and uninhibited, are the best, but this is not something one can plan for and it may be necessary to work through many iterations before one achieves the desired result. I see the drawings as part of the design process: one just has to keep going until it looks right.

.

I chose to start this book with recent projects, closer to my thoughts. The Maggie's Centre in Oxford, for example, is a small project but intense in its architectural expression and detailing. Its concept, related to a 'tree house', emerged from the particular constraints caused by a slope across the site and my interpretation of the brief, which required the interior spaces to have close contact with nature. My early sketches show a simplistic interpretation of this, which later took shape as the concept was refined, leading to drawings that are

remarkably similar to the actual building completed in September 2014.

This is followed by an ongoing major project, the Crown Hotel, Sydney, in which my very first exploratory sketches led to the narrative that helped win the competition; a narrative that formed the basis for the final architectural design as it progressed to construction. Illustrative sketches explore more detailed aspects of the design for different areas of the building, such as the veil of marble tracery that encloses the podium and canopies at street level.

Early options for a tower in the City of London, codenamed Prussian Blue, are followed by our scheme for the new research building and cafe at the Dyson headquarters at Malmesbury. This project continues my close association with the inventor Sir James Dyson CBE, which started back in 1994, when his amazingly successful company was just starting to take off. My sketches for that first building are included elsewhere in this book. Other recently completed projects, such as the Worthing Pools, now known as Splashpoint, and the Mary Rose Museum at Portsmouth Harbour, are included with conceptual sketches and sample details from my sketchbooks. It was a great privilege to be involved in the design of a new museum to house Henry VIII's favourite warship and all its treasures. Early sketches from 2005 show the emergence of the concept, which was developed with the team over several years until its completion in 2013. A final phase is planned for 2016, when the ship will have dried out completely.

Many other projects and competition entries are included, too, some built and others that fell by the wayside. These tend to represent either strong

design ideas, or interesting drawing techniques illustrating the diversity of our projects. A favourite among these was *Landscape to Portrait*, an installation created for the Annenberg Courtyard during the Royal Academy's 2012 Summer Exhibition. The project, which I designed with my wife Diana and our son Dominic while I was at home recovering from an operation, coincided with my commission to hang the Architecture Room inside the summer show. It took on special importance because it was the year of the Queen's Diamond Jubilee and of the London Olympics. *Landscape to Portrait* was completed just in time for a major royal reception that was attended by 700 top arts celebrities, all waiting in the courtyard for the Queen to arrive.

Bridges, an important part of the practice's workload, are overseen mostly by my partner Jim Eyre, but I have included some of those projects I have been involved with. Two have special significance for me: the Challenge of Materials Bridge at the Science Museum, London, which I created with Paul Baker and the engineer Bryn Bird, and also the Seine Bridge competition, which I worked on with Sebastien Ricard and Chris Wise.

Representing a completely different sector, the Guangzhou International Finance Center was a successful international competition win in 2005 that went on to be constructed. At 440 m high, it is still one of the world's tallest buildings. For this project, I have included some early sketches and an illustration of the completed building that I drew during a quiet moment on the occasion of the official opening in 2012.

I have selected only a few of the many drawings in my sketchbooks that illustrate the design concepts of millennium-era cultural projects, such as Magna, Explore@Bristol and the Swansea Waterfront Museum. These mark an important turning point, when the practice was starting to take off. The two Jubilee Line projects – Stratford Market Depot and Stratford Station – are included as the first major projects we undertook in the early 1990s, when the practice was still called Chris Wilkinson Architects.

•

Publishing one's sketchbooks is rather like baring one's soul, a decision that is not to be taken lightly. One of the reasons I decided to go ahead with it was to emphasise the importance of drawing in architecture. For me, and for generations of architects before me, drawing has been an essential part of the design process. Now, with the almost universal use of computers, this can no longer be said to be true. However, I strongly believe that the process of drawing enhances the creative act. There is something about eye–brain–hand coordination that seems to stimulate ideas, just as it serves to communicate them. It can also be said that although a CGI rendering conveys a design in a superbly accurate way, a freehand sketch can often express the emotions and thinking behind a concept.

I hope drawing will always remain an important part of the architectural process.

CN 06

twisting geometry

Tree House

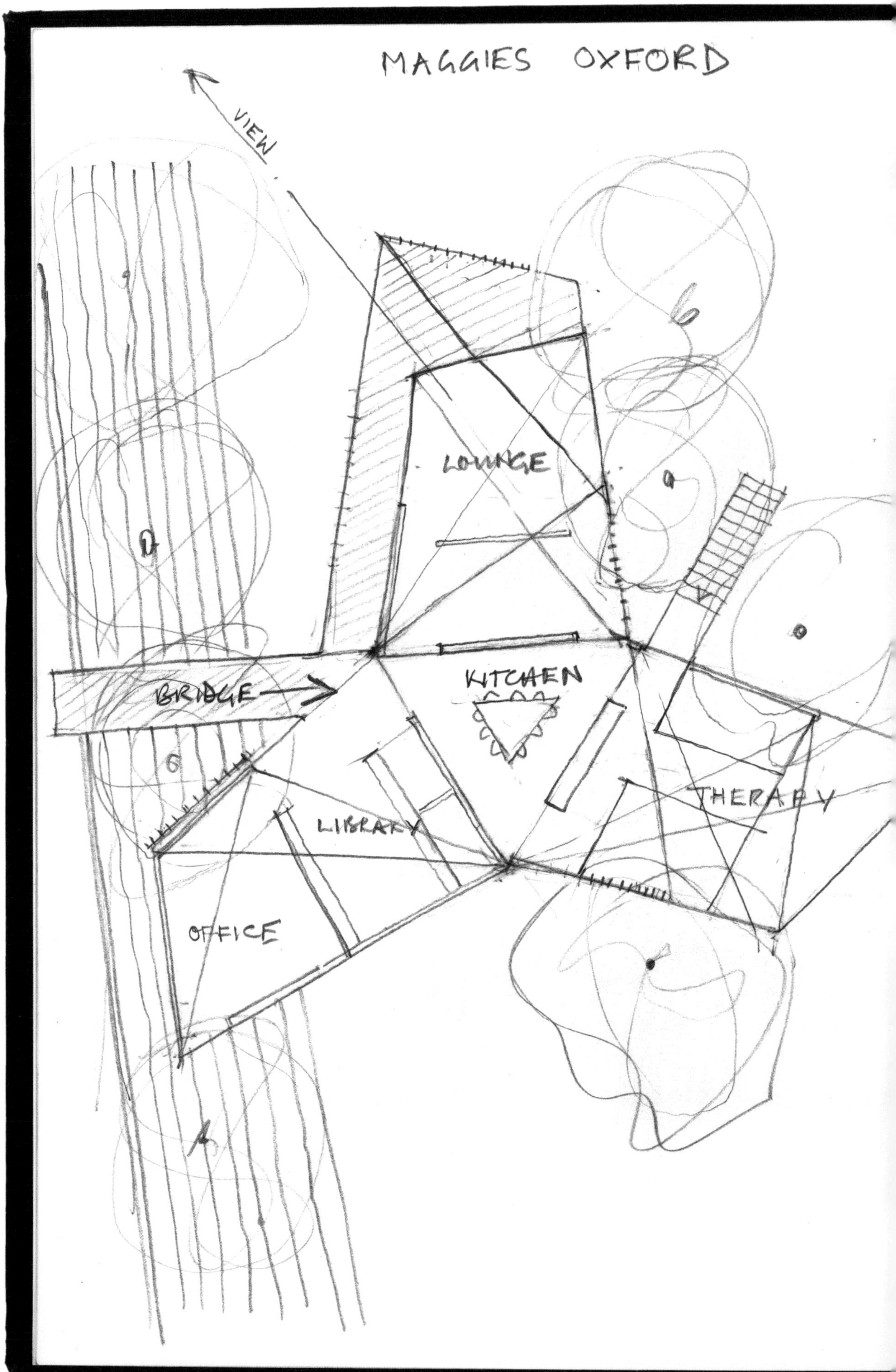

MAGGIES OXFORD

VIEW

LOUNGE

BRIDGE →

KITCHEN

THERAPY

LIBRARY

OFFICE

14|15

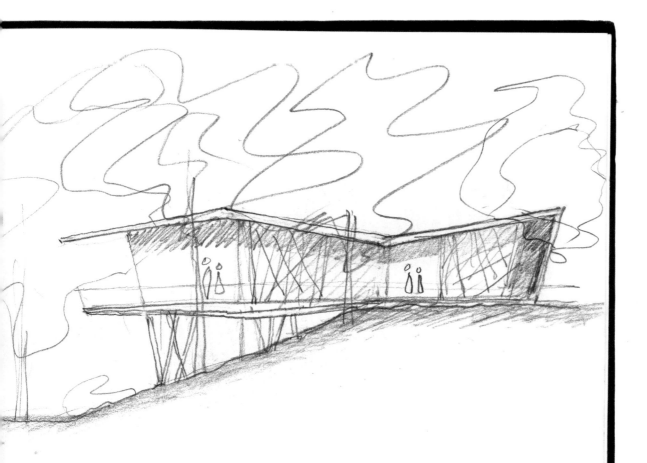

'Tree House' on the edge of the
Churchill Hospital with tripartite
plan. Access by bridge from
the Oncology car park.
Folded planes of triangular geometry
fabricated in cross ply laminated
timber.

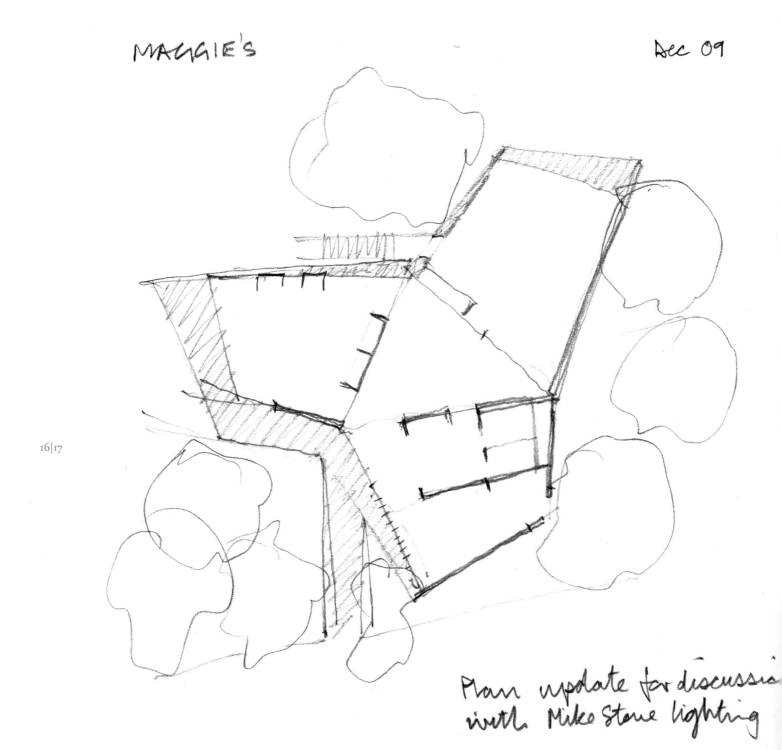

Plan update for discussion
with Mike Stone lighting

TRIANGULAR TABLE FOR MAGGIES

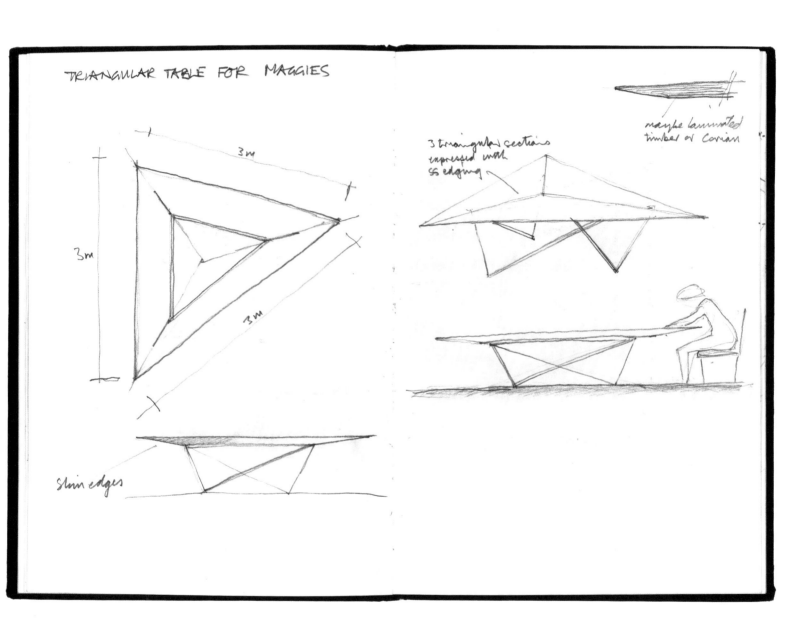

3m

3m

3m

stain edges

3 triangular sections
expressed with
SS edging

maybe laminated
timber or Corian

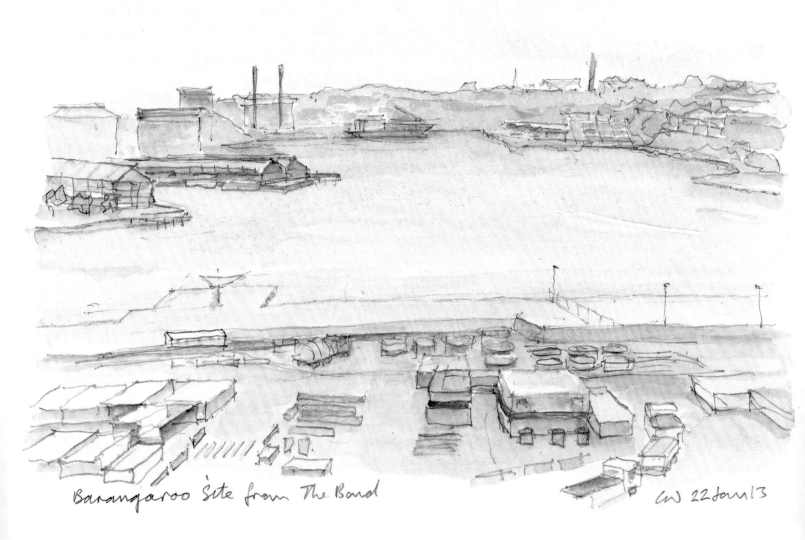

Barangaroo Site from The Bond   CW 22 Jan 13

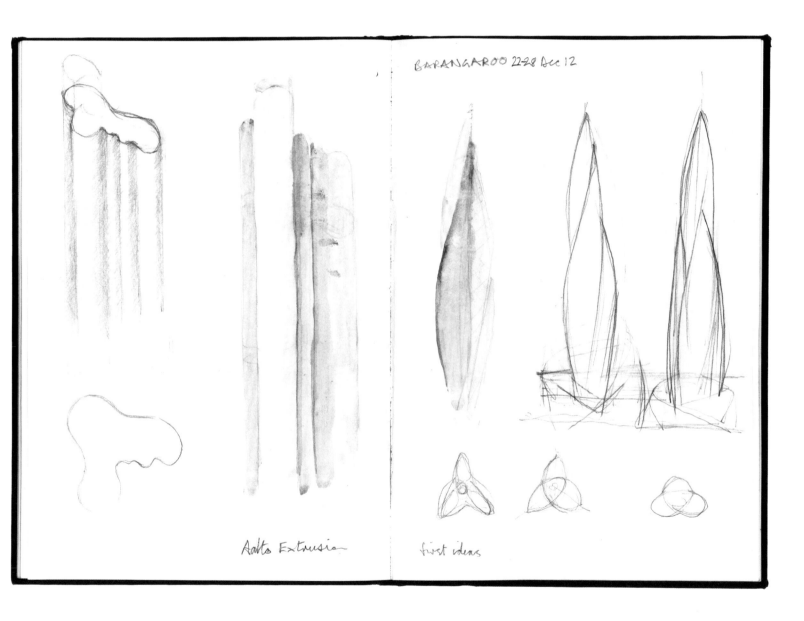

BARANGAROO 2228 Dec 12

Aalto Extrusion

first ideas

Barangaroo concepts
7-11 Jan 13

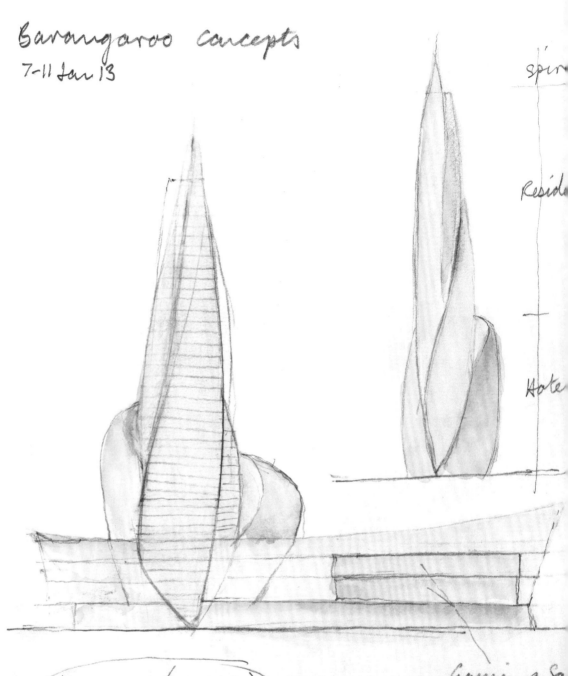

Spir

Reside

Hote

Gaming Sa

'leaves / Petals'
Sculptural forms emiate from central cor
organic growth of leaves/petals
contrasts with rectangular surroundings
need to maximing views and terraces

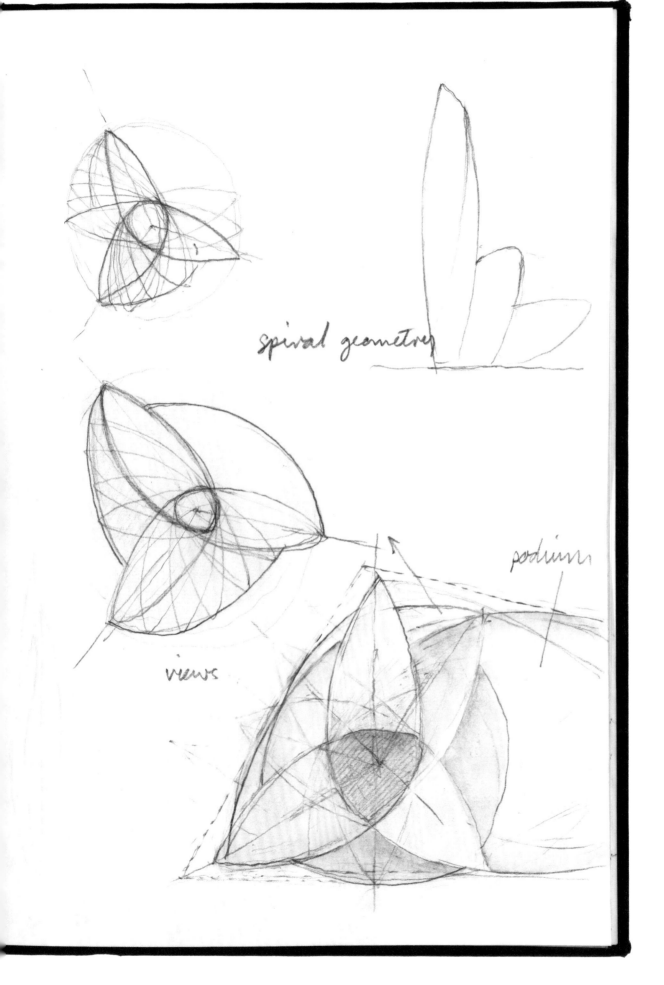

spiral geometry

views

podium

BARANGAROO   Roof studies with an extra petal
8 April

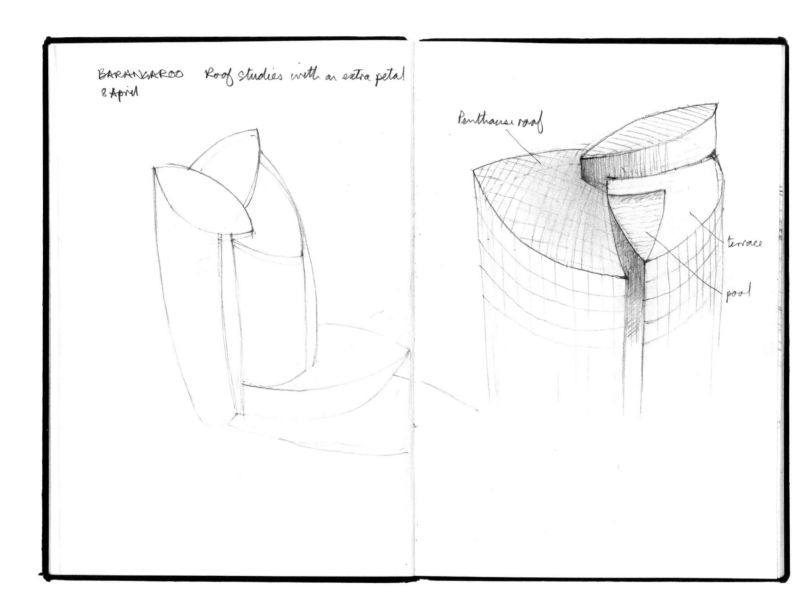

Penthouse roof

terrace

pool

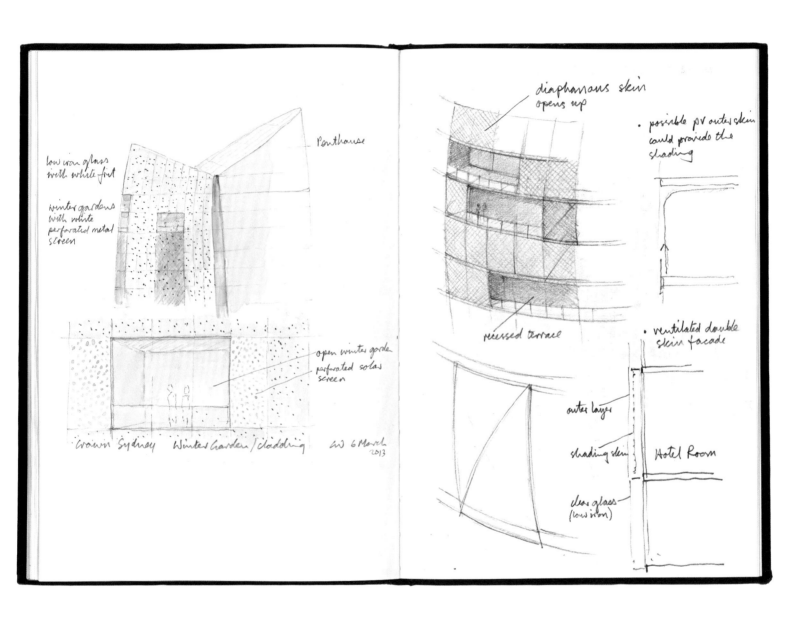

low iron glass
with white frit

winter gardens
with white
perforated metal
screen

Penthouse

open winter garde
perforated solar
screen

Crown Sydney   Winter Garden / cladding   LW 6 March 2013

diaphanous skin
opens up

recessed terrace

· possible pv outer skin
could provide the
shading

· ventilated double
skin facade

outer layer

shading skin

clear glass
(low iron)

Hotel Room

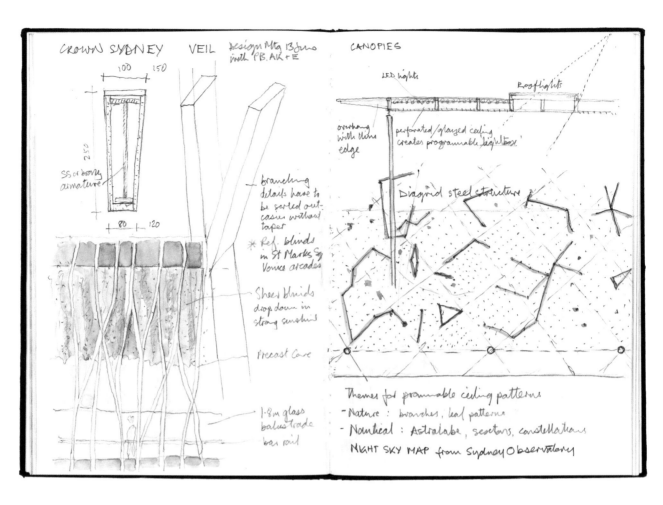

CROWN SYDNEY   VEIL   design Mtg 13 Juno
                       with PB, AK + E

CANOPIES

100   150

250

SS or bronze armature

80   120

branching details have to be sorted out—cases without taper

* Ref. blinds in St Marks Sq Venice arcades

Sheer blinds drop down in strong sunshine

Precast Core

1.8m glass balustrade bar rail

LED lights

Rooflights

overhang with thin edge

perforated/glazed ceiling creates programmable lightbox

Diagrid steel structure

Themes for programmable ceiling patterns
- Nature : branches, leaf patterns
- Nautical : Astrolabe, sextants, constellations
NIGHT SKY MAP from Sydney Observatory

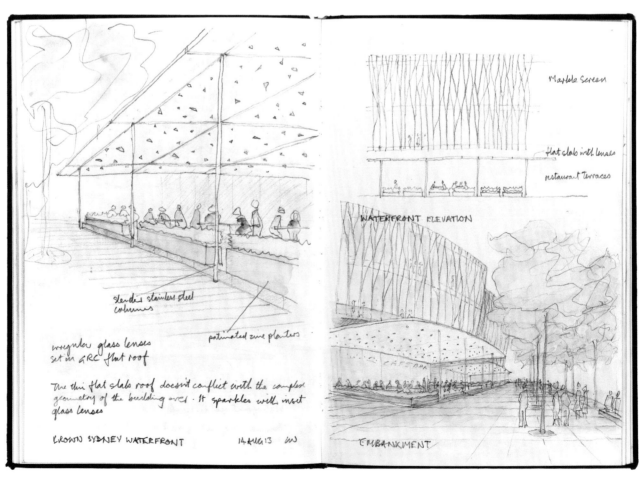

slender stainless steel columns

patinated zinc planters

irregular glass lenses set in GRC flat roof

The thin flat slab roof doesn't conflict with the complex geometry of the building over. It sparkles with inset glass lenses

CROWN SYDNEY WATERFRONT   14 AUG 13

Marble Screen

flat slab with lenses

restaurant terraces

WATERFRONT ELEVATION

EMBANKMENT

Idea for West Elevation to Podium June 13

laser cut white marble
Veil

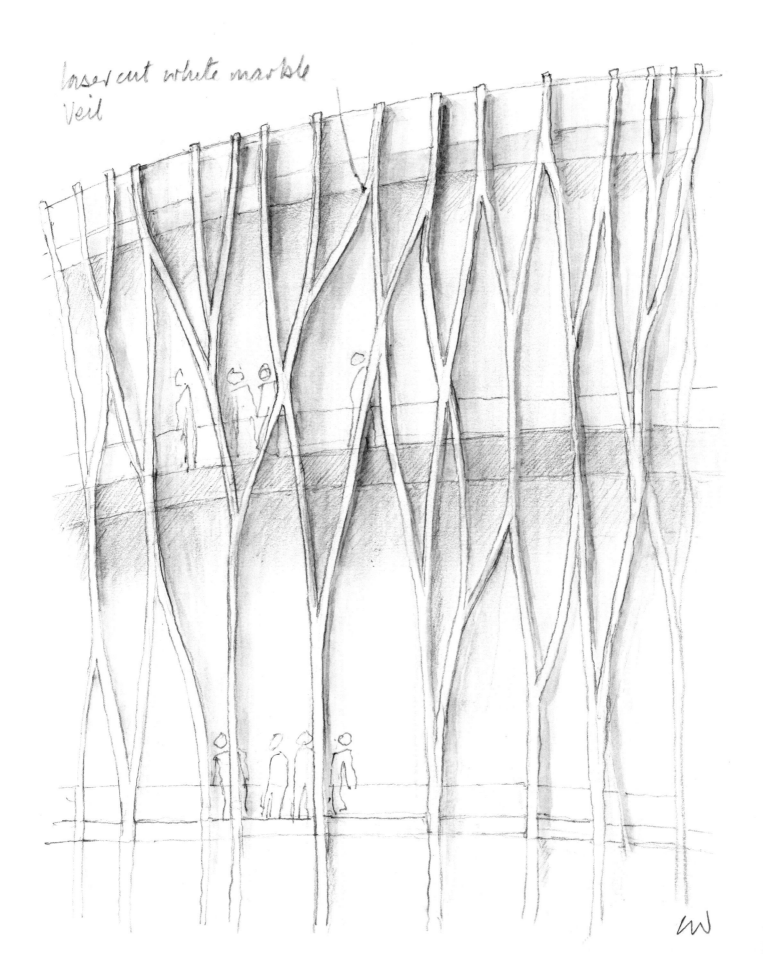

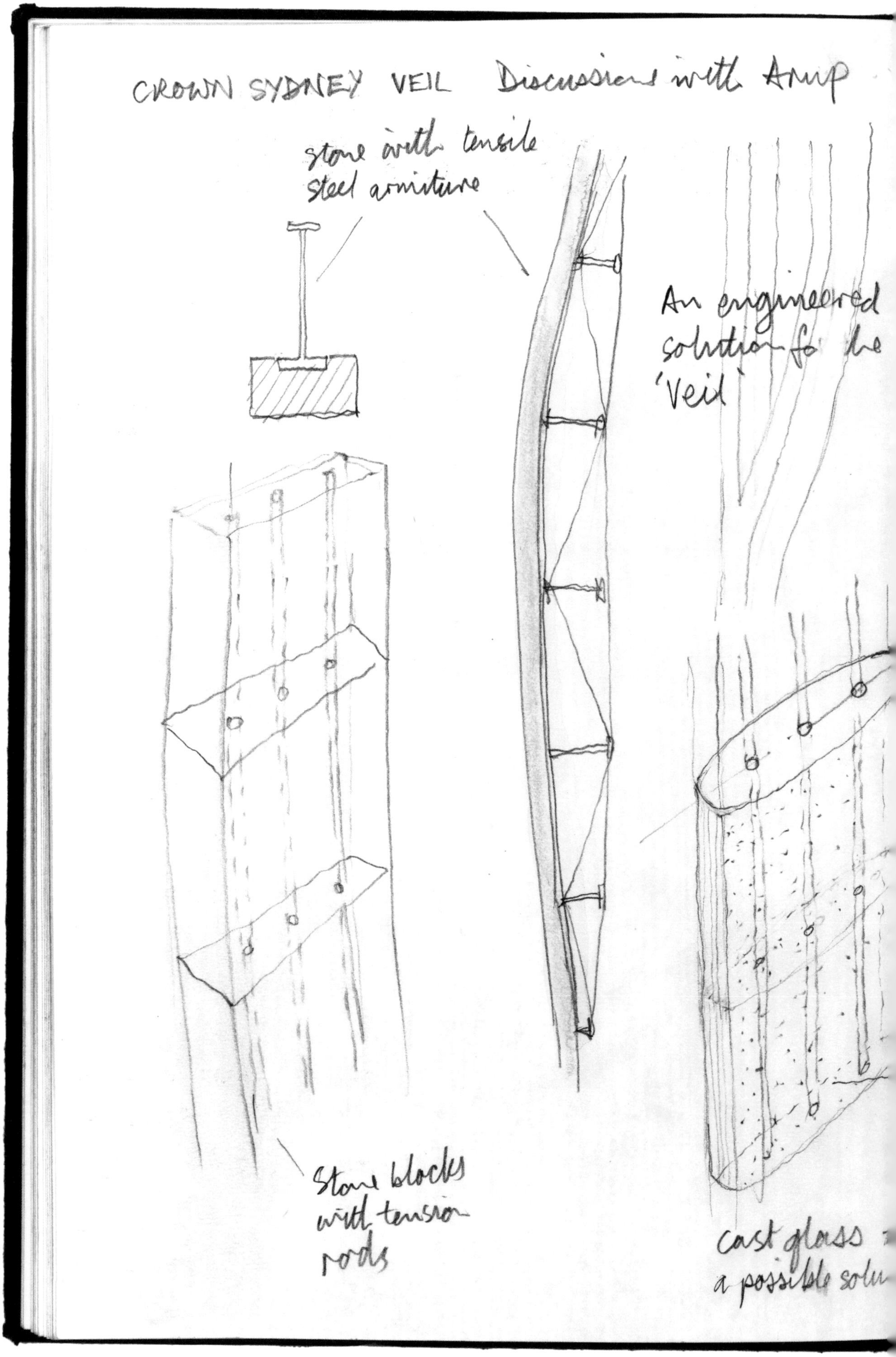

CROWN SYDNEY VEIL   Discussions with Arup

stone with tensile
steel armature

An engineered
solution for the
'veil'

Stone blocks
with tension
rods

cast glass –
a possible solu...

July 14

High Tech Gothic

sheer blinds

stone ribs
with tensvia
structure

glass
balustrade!

blinds like
St Marks Sq
arcades

cast glass
catches the light
and could glow
at night with
inset light

OPTIONS : 1. stone — quality, history
make use of latest technology

2. glass — fresh + light
innovation

3. GRC — reconstituted stone
casting in large sections

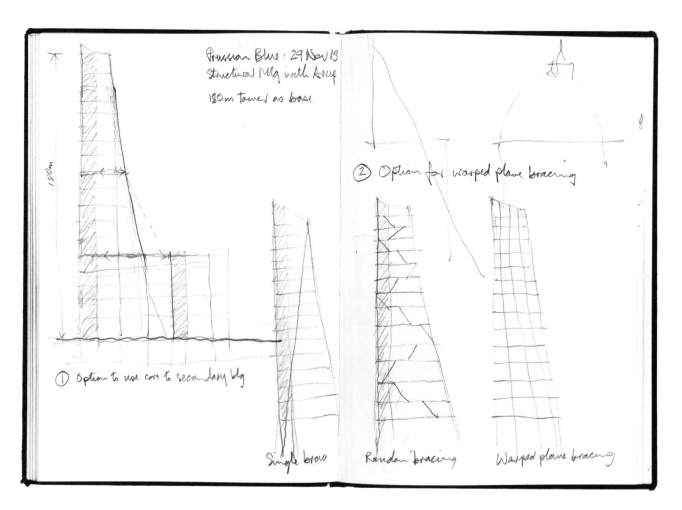

Prussian Blue: 29 Nov 13
Structural Mtg with Arup

180m tower as base

① Option to use core to secondary bldg

② Option for warped plane bracing

Single brace   Random bracing   Warped plane bracing

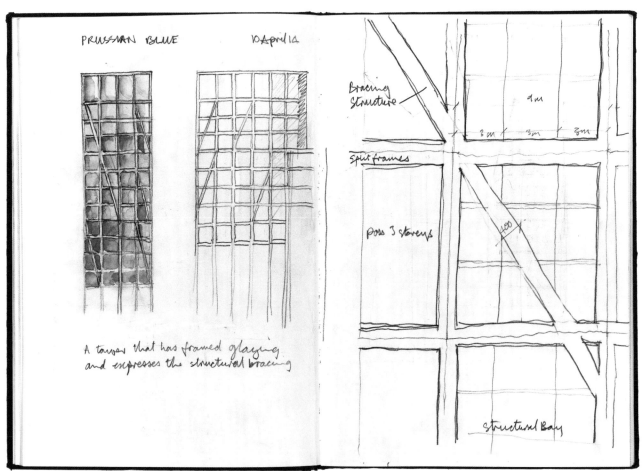

PRUSSIAN BLUE   10 April 14

A tower that has framed glazing
and expresses the structural bracing

Bracing
Structure

Split frames

Poss 3 storeys

9m

3m   3m   3m

400

structural Bay

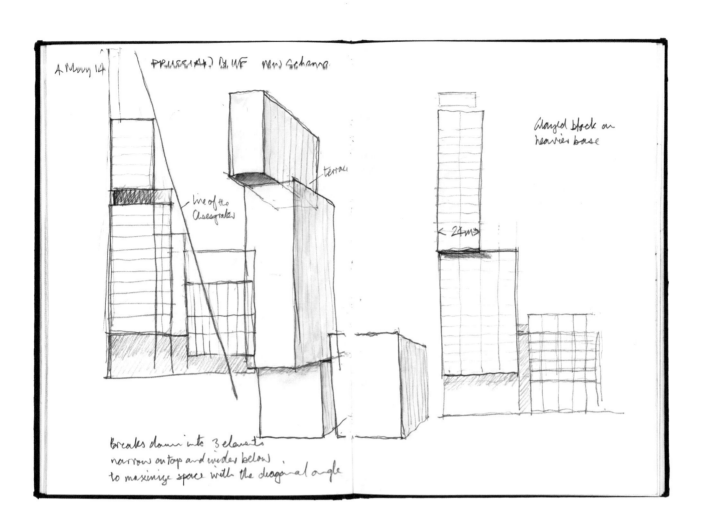

A May 14   PRUSSIAN BLUE   Mw Scheme

Glazed block on heavier base

terrace

line of the Cheesegrater

< 24m >

Breaks down into 3 elements
narrow on top and wider below
to maximize space with the diagonal angle

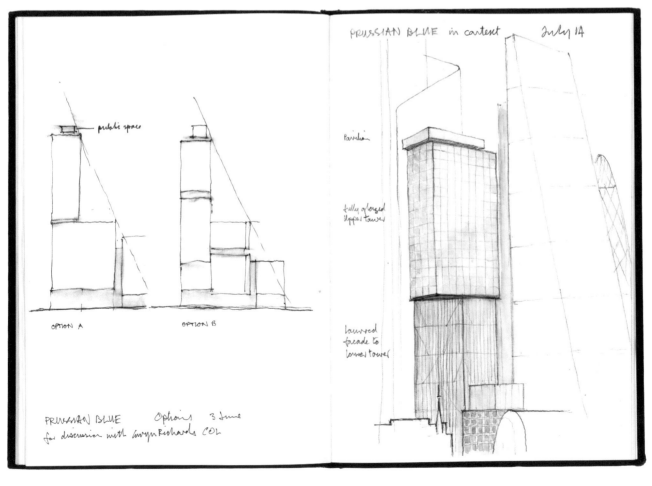

PRUSSIAN BLUE in context   July 14

Pavilion

fully glazed upper tower

louvred facade to lower tower

public space

OPTION A   OPTION B

PRUSSIAN BLUE   Options 3 June
for discussion with Gwyn Richards COL

BRISTOL ARENA COMPETITION   18 Jan 15

Transparency of the bowl through the glazed
cladding, animated by 'people' on the stairs
and concourses

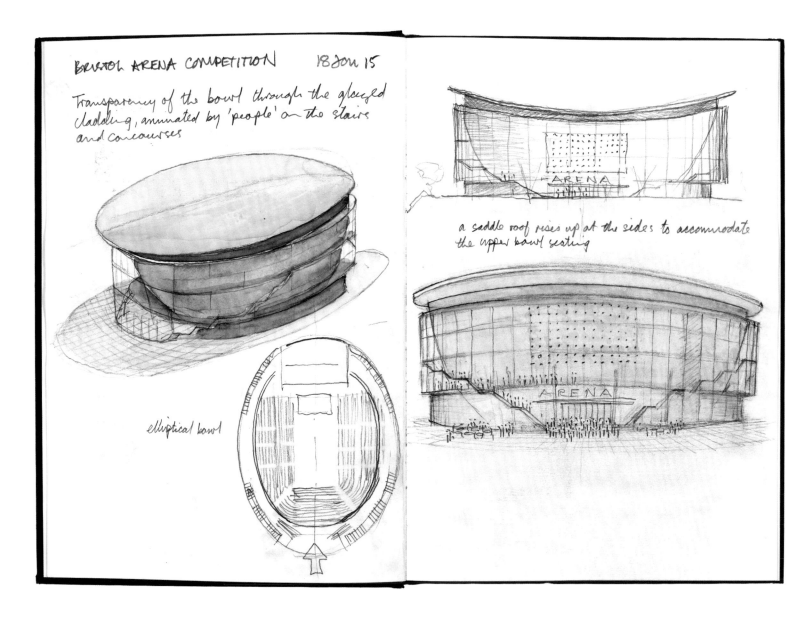

elliptical bowl

a saddle roof rises up at the sides to accommodate
the upper bowl seating

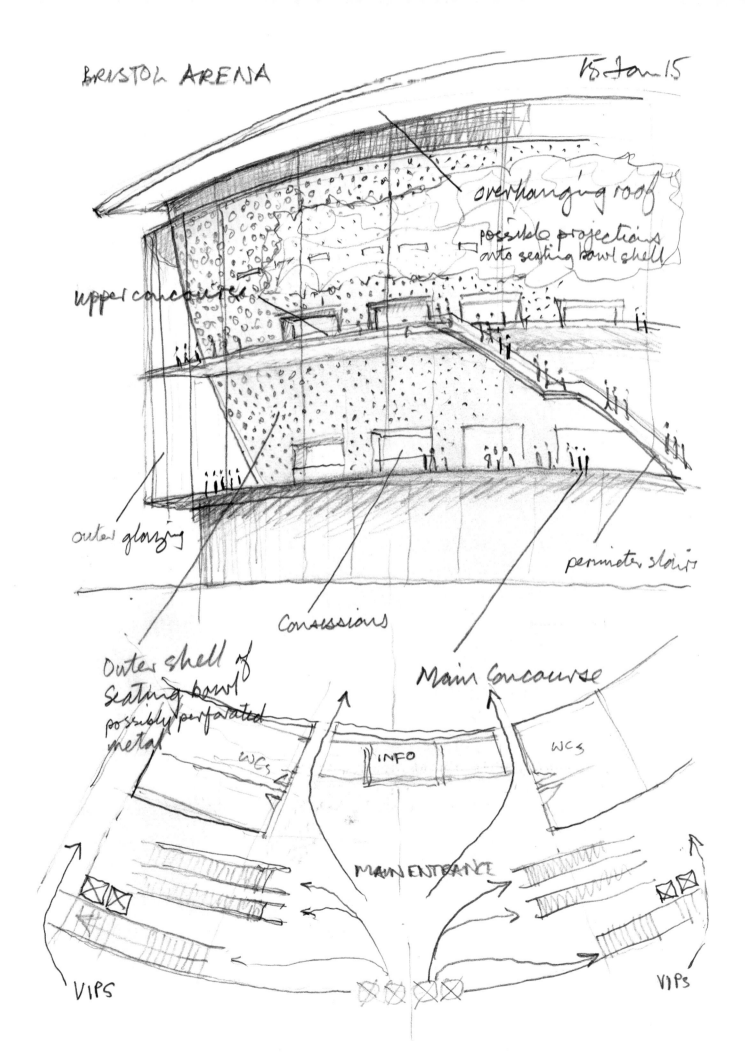

BRISTOL ARENA

15 Jan 15

overhanging roof

possible projections
onto seating bowl shell

upper concourse

outer glazing

perimeter stairs

Concessions

Main Concourse

Outer shell of
Seating bowl
possibly perforated
metal

WCs

INFO

WCs

MAIN ENTRANCE

VIPS

VIPS

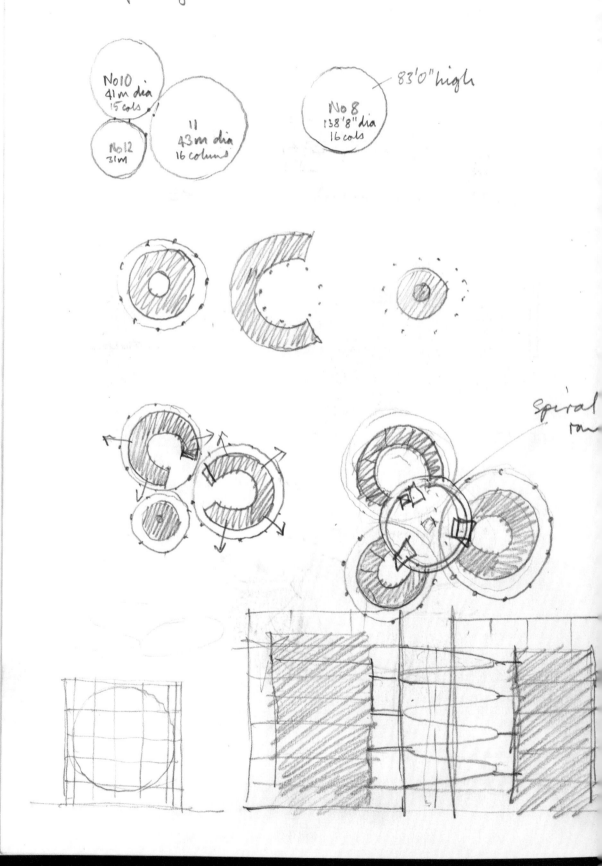

No10 dia
41m dia
15 cols

No12
31m

11
43m dia
16 columns

No 8
138'8" dia
16 cols

83'0" high

spiral
ra

32|33

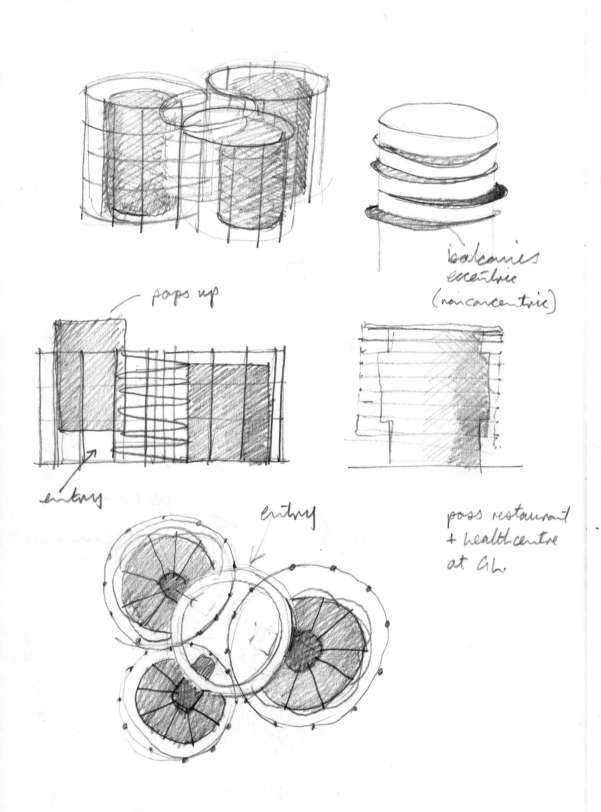

balconies
eccentric
(nonconcentric)

pops up

entry

entry

pass restaurant
+ health centre
at G.L.

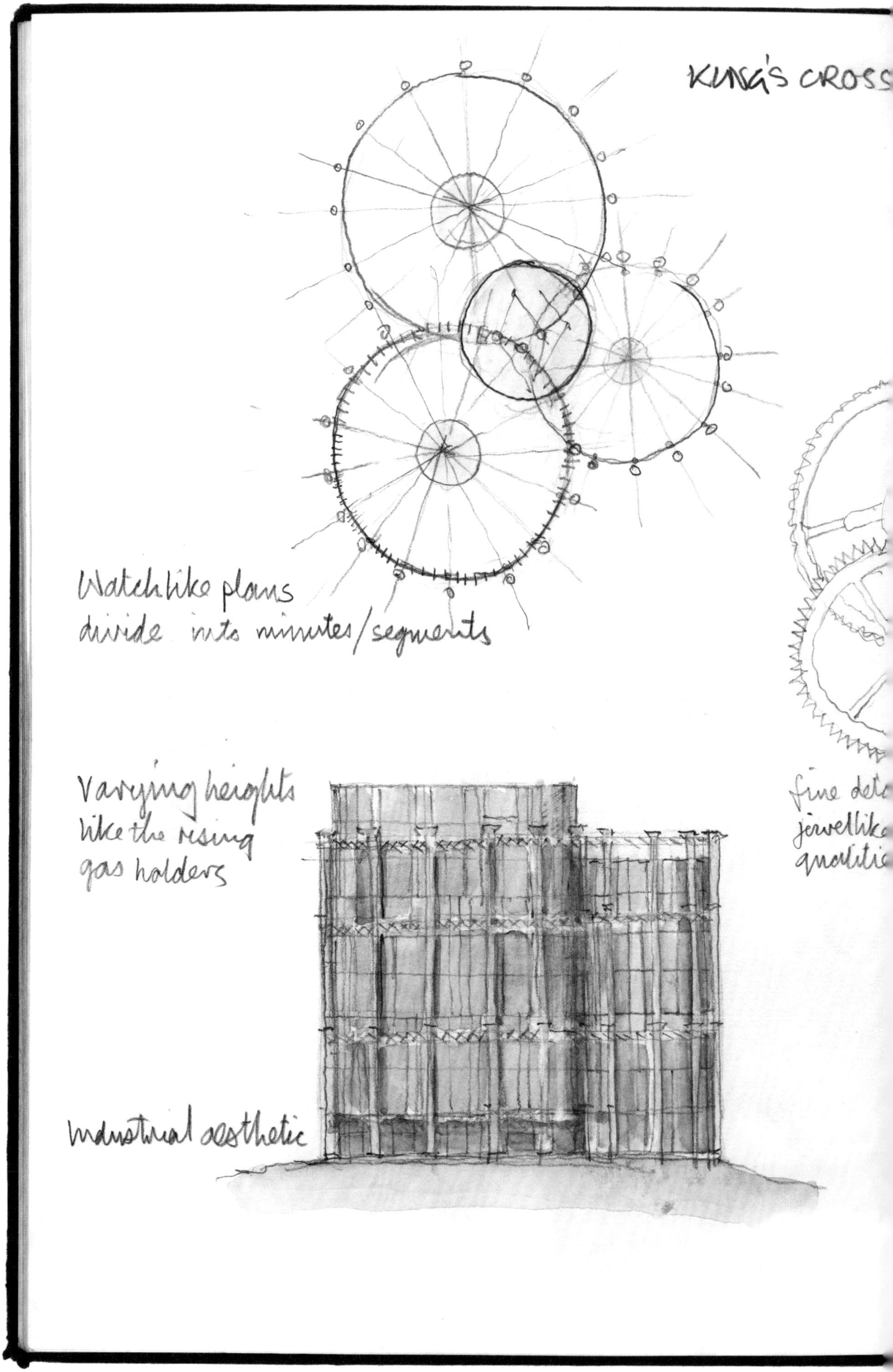

Watchlike plans
divide into minutes/segments

Varying heights
like the rising
gas holders

industrial aesthetic

fine deta
jewellike
qualities

ASHOLDERS   Dec13

brass strips

inset balconies

sliding folding
perforated screens

DYSON 9   R&D   14 Feb 14

A reductive box

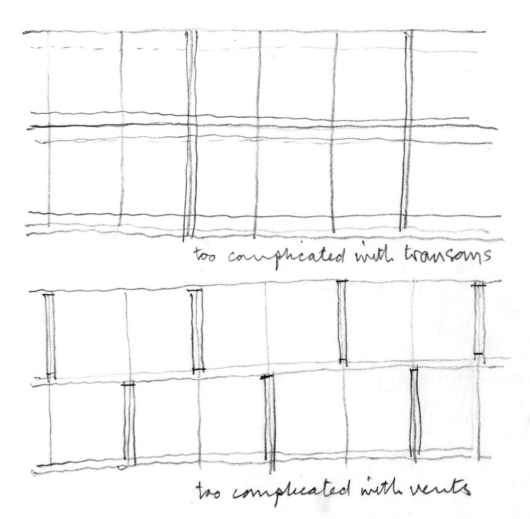

too complicated with transoms

too complicated with vents

36|37

large glass panels
silver mirrored finish

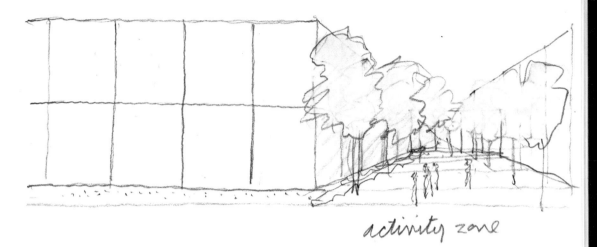

activity zone

Keep it simple!

Battersea Power Station

LW 1 Feb 13

MARY ROSE MUSEUM

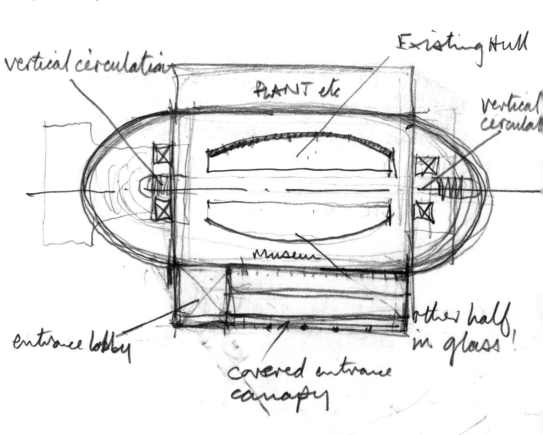

vertical circulation

Existing Hull

vertical circulation

PLANT etc

museum

entrance lobby

other half in glass!

covered entrance canopy

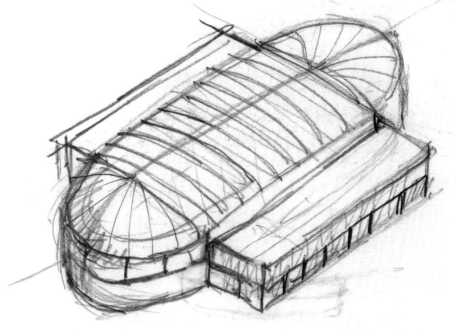

Galleries   Mary Rose   mussel shape
                          enclosure
                                     Galleries

                                     3 levels
                                     related to
                                     the decks

- Start with image of the Hull
- build up the new elements
- circulation   interpretation
- diagram of the various activities
- the building   — conservation
- the site   marine archaeology
- the team (composite images)
- DESTINATION

5.0pm 4th April

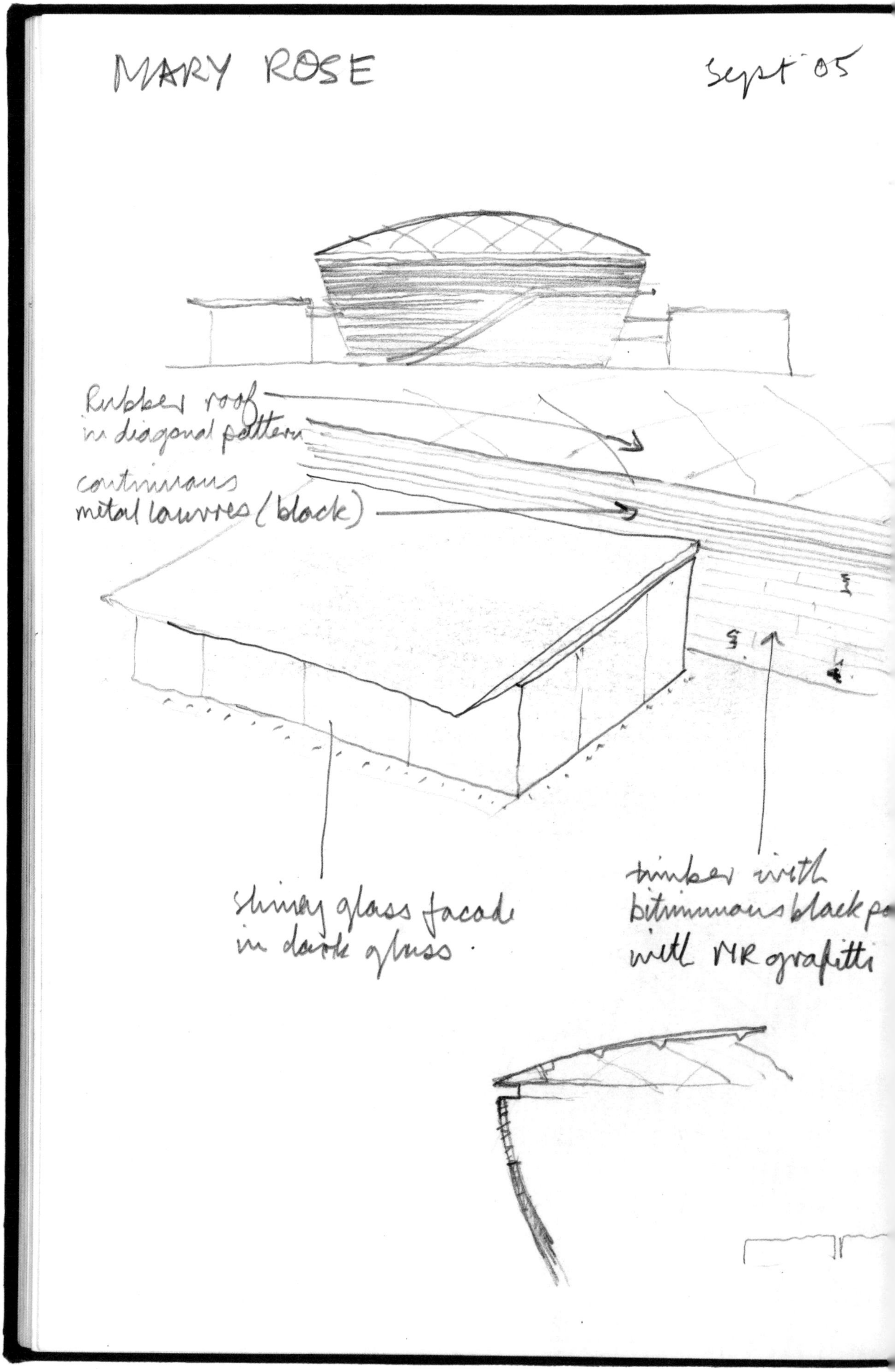

Rubber roof
in diagonal pattern

continuous
metal louvres (black)

shiny glass facade
in dark glass.

timber with
bituminous black paint
with MR grafitti

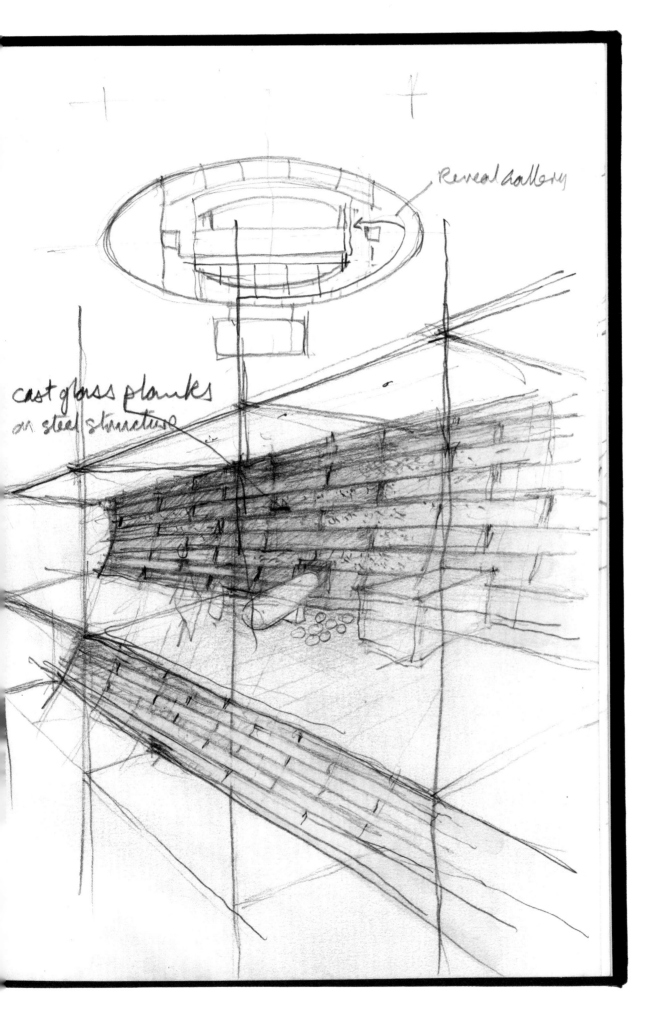

Reveal Gallery

cast glass planks
on steel structure

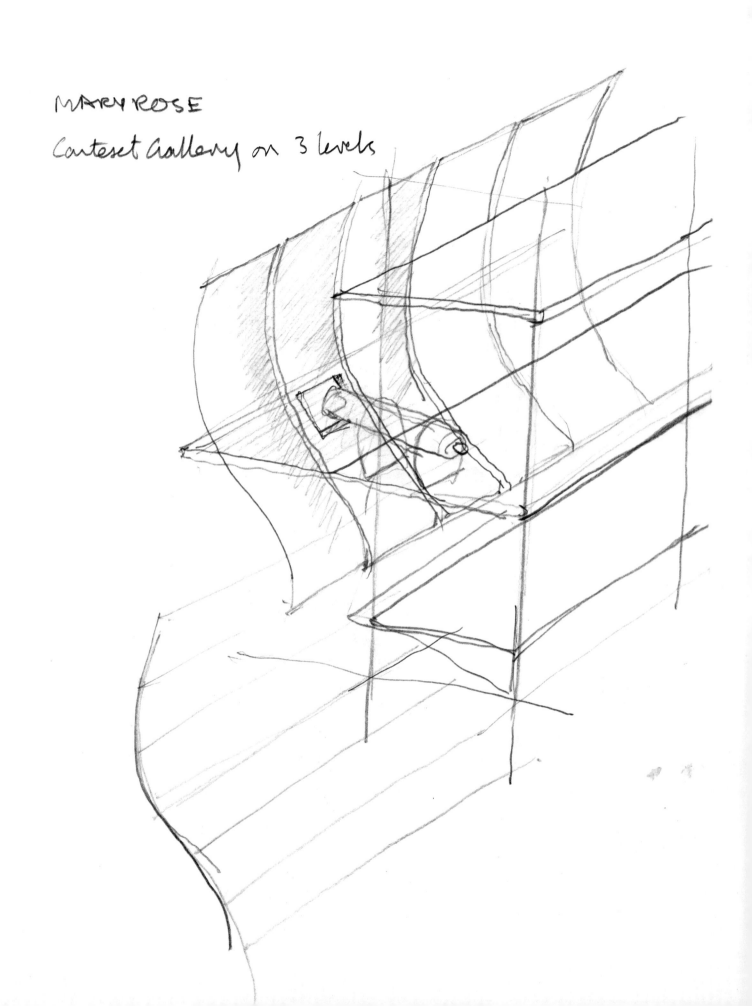

MARY ROSE

Context Gallery on 3 levels

Mary Rose alongside HMS Victory

Opened April 2013

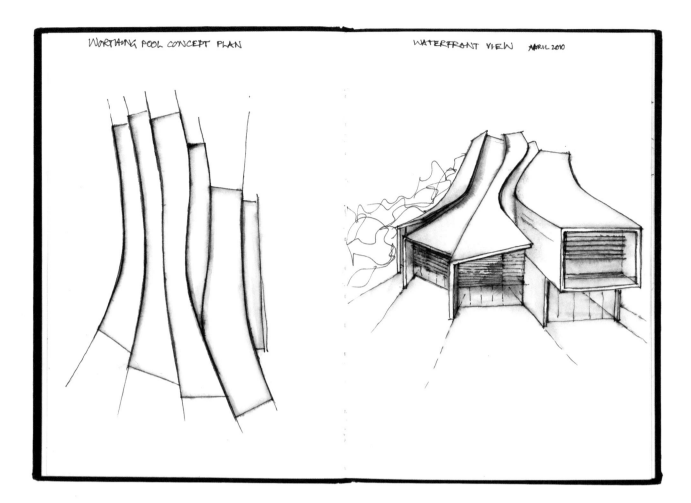

46|47

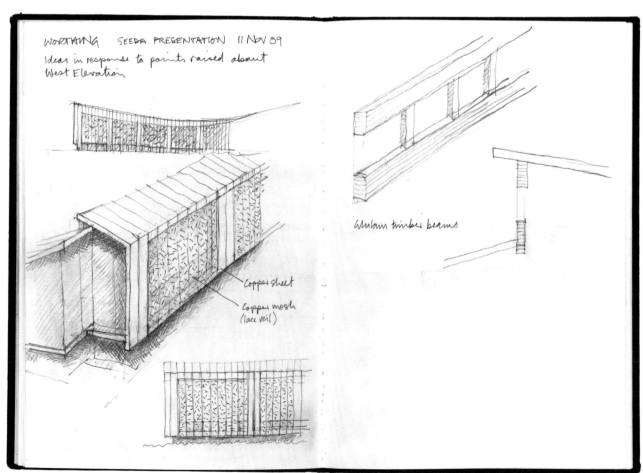

WORTHING   SEEDA PRESENTATION   11 NOV 09
Ideas in response to points raised about
West Elevation

Copper sheet

Copper mesh
(lace veil)

Glulam timber beams

WORTHING POOL.

Fluid forms of Worthing

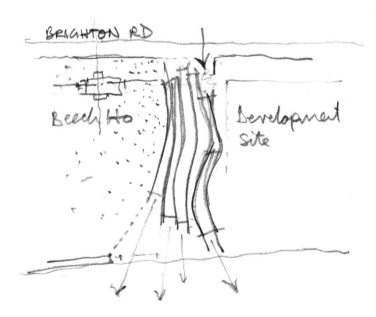

BRIGHTON RD

Beach Ho

Development
Site

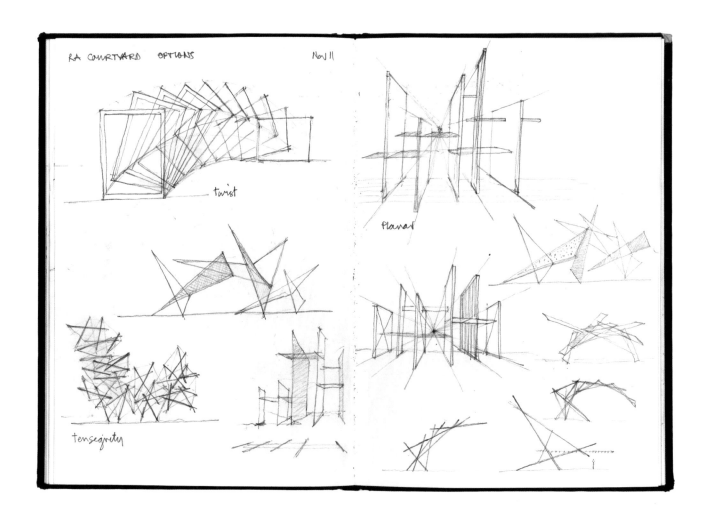

RA COURTYARD OPTIONS   Nov 11

twist

Planar

tensegrity

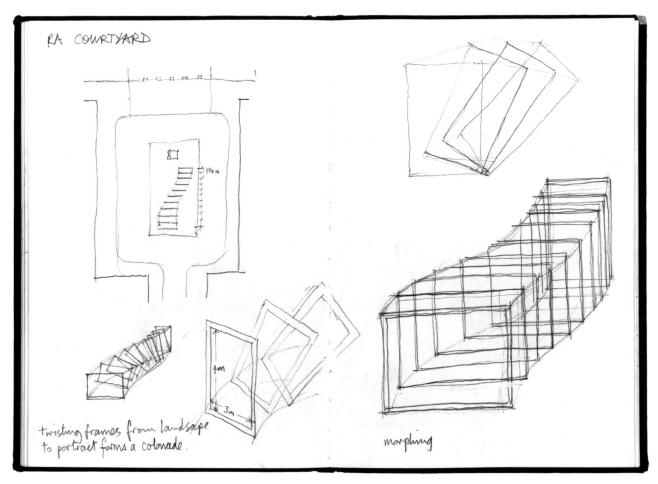

RA COURTYARD

1½ m

4m

3m

twisting frames from landscape
to portrait forms a colonade.

morphing

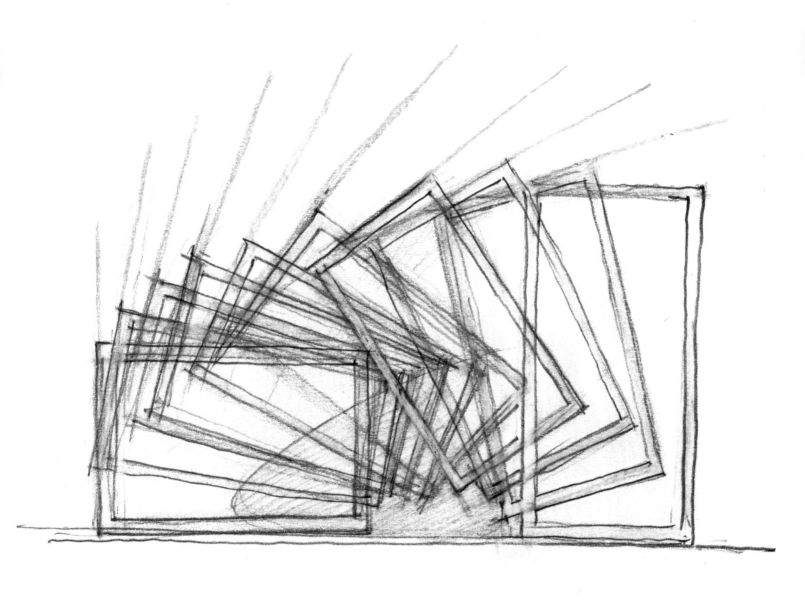

LANDSCAPE TO PORTRAIT

Siemens' Urban Sustainability Centre is a showcase
for sustainable design.

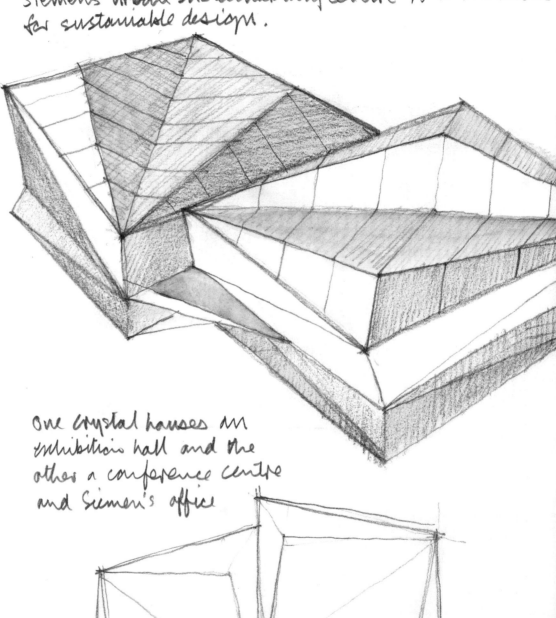

One crystal houses an
exhibition hall and the
other a conference centre
and Siemen's office

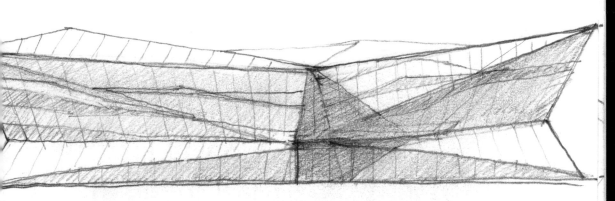

VIEW FROM THE DOCK

TWO INTERLOCKING PARALLELOGRAM
FORMS CUT INTO MULTIPLE TRIANGULAR
FACETS. ITS CRYSTALLINE GEOMETRY
CATCHES THE LIGHT FROM THE WATER
IN DIFFERENT WAYS, WHICH IS
EMPHASISED BY A VARYING PALLET
OF REFLECTIVE AND TRANSPARENT
GLAZING.

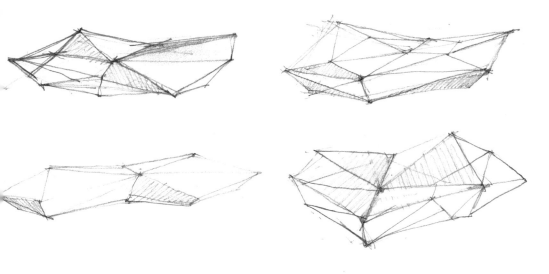

crystalline sculptural form

Competition entry for 2012 London Games

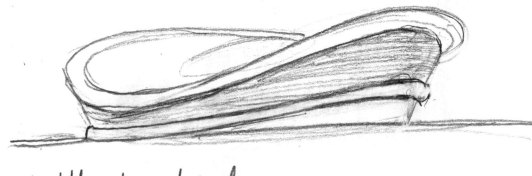

saddle shaped roof

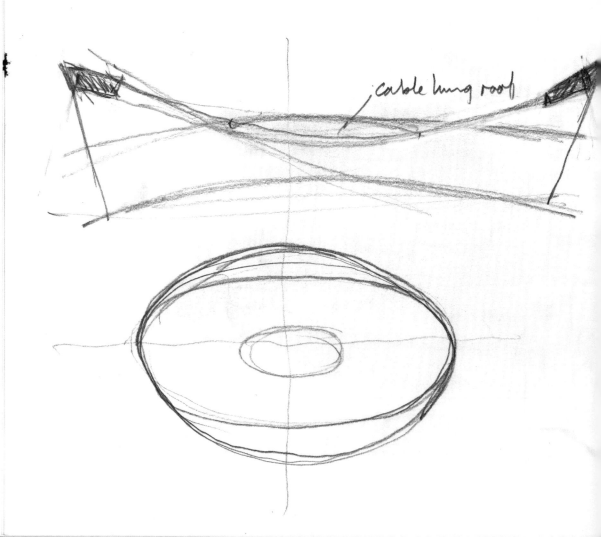

cable hung roof

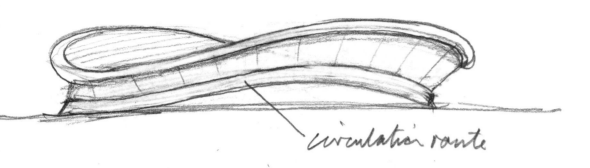

circulation route

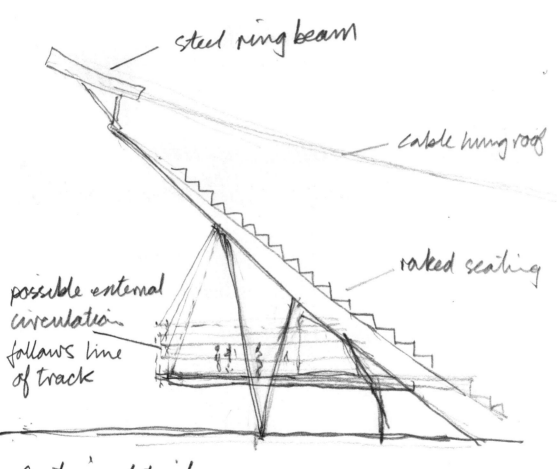

steel ring beam

cable hung roof

raked seating

possible external
circulation
follows line
of track

Section detail

GUANGZHOU WEST TOWER

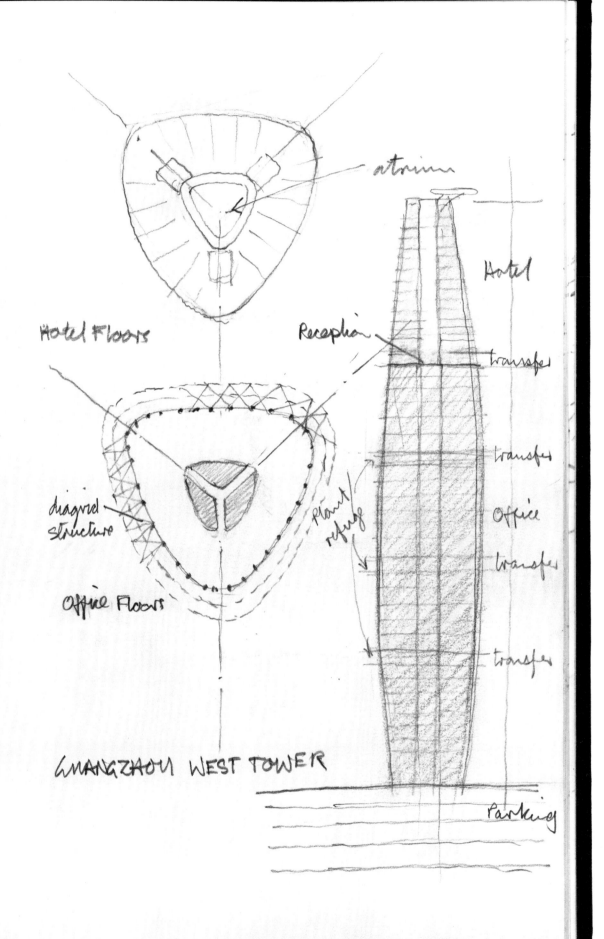

atrium

Hotel Floors

Reception

Hotel

transfer

diagrid
structure

Plant
refuge

transfer

Office Floors

Office

transfer

GUANGZHOU WEST TOWER

transfer

Parking

GUANGZHOU TOWER   Sept 05

Trocoid

48m

6 - 8 storeys

12m

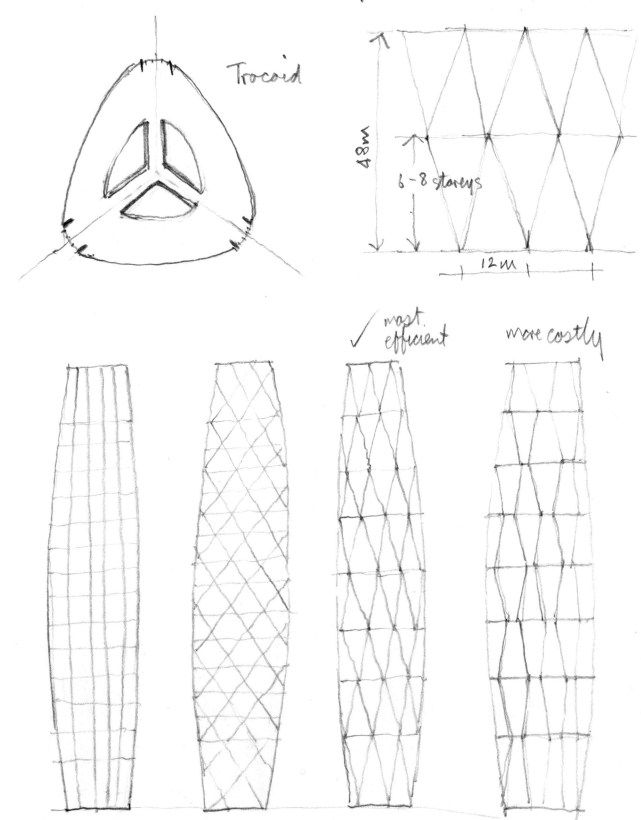

✓ most efficient   more costly

likely steel tubes filled with concrete

Guangzhou IFC

27 Sept 12

GRETNA MONUMENT   Mar 11

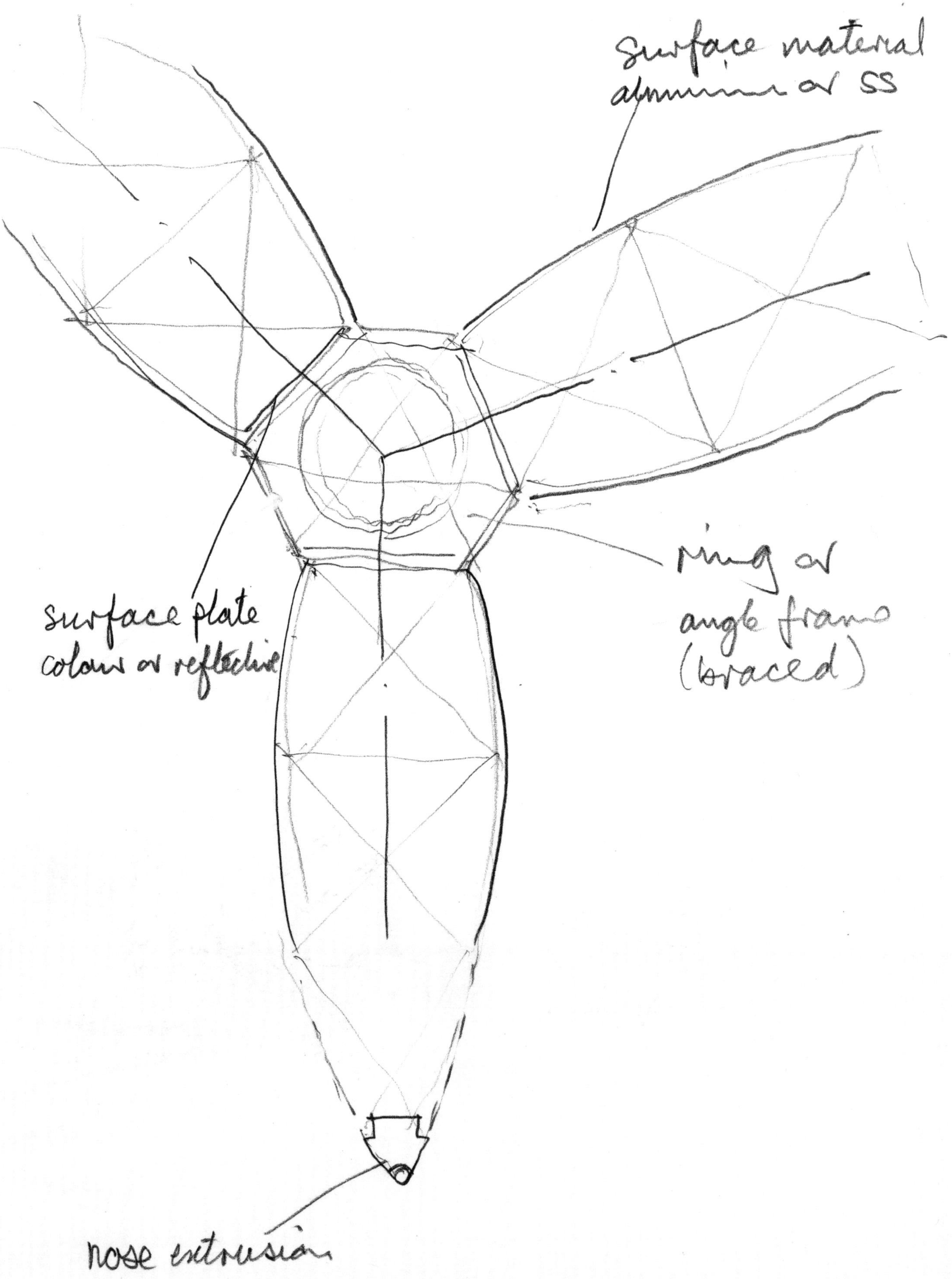

surface material
aluminium or SS

surface plate
colour or reflective

ring or
angle frame
(braced)

nose extrusion

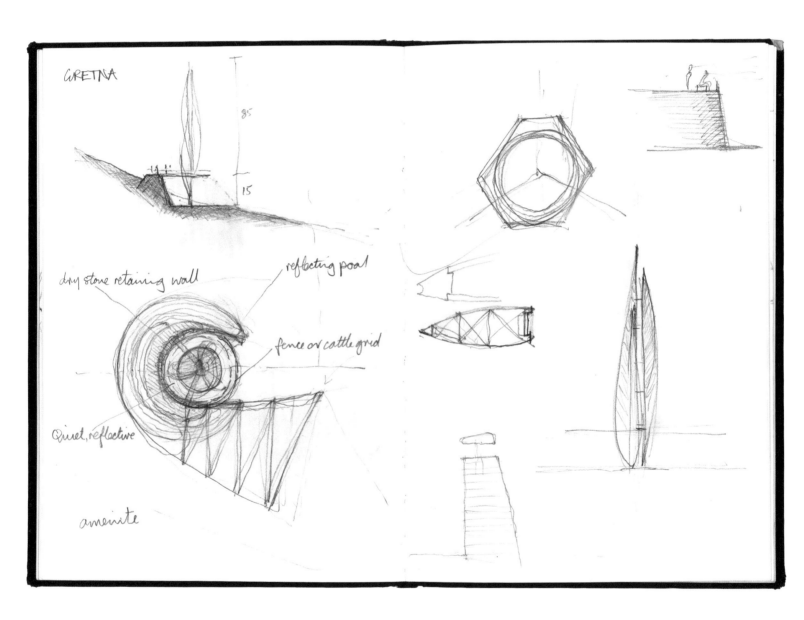

GRETNA

85

15

dry stone retaining wall

reflecting pool

fence or cattle grid

Quiet, reflective

amenite

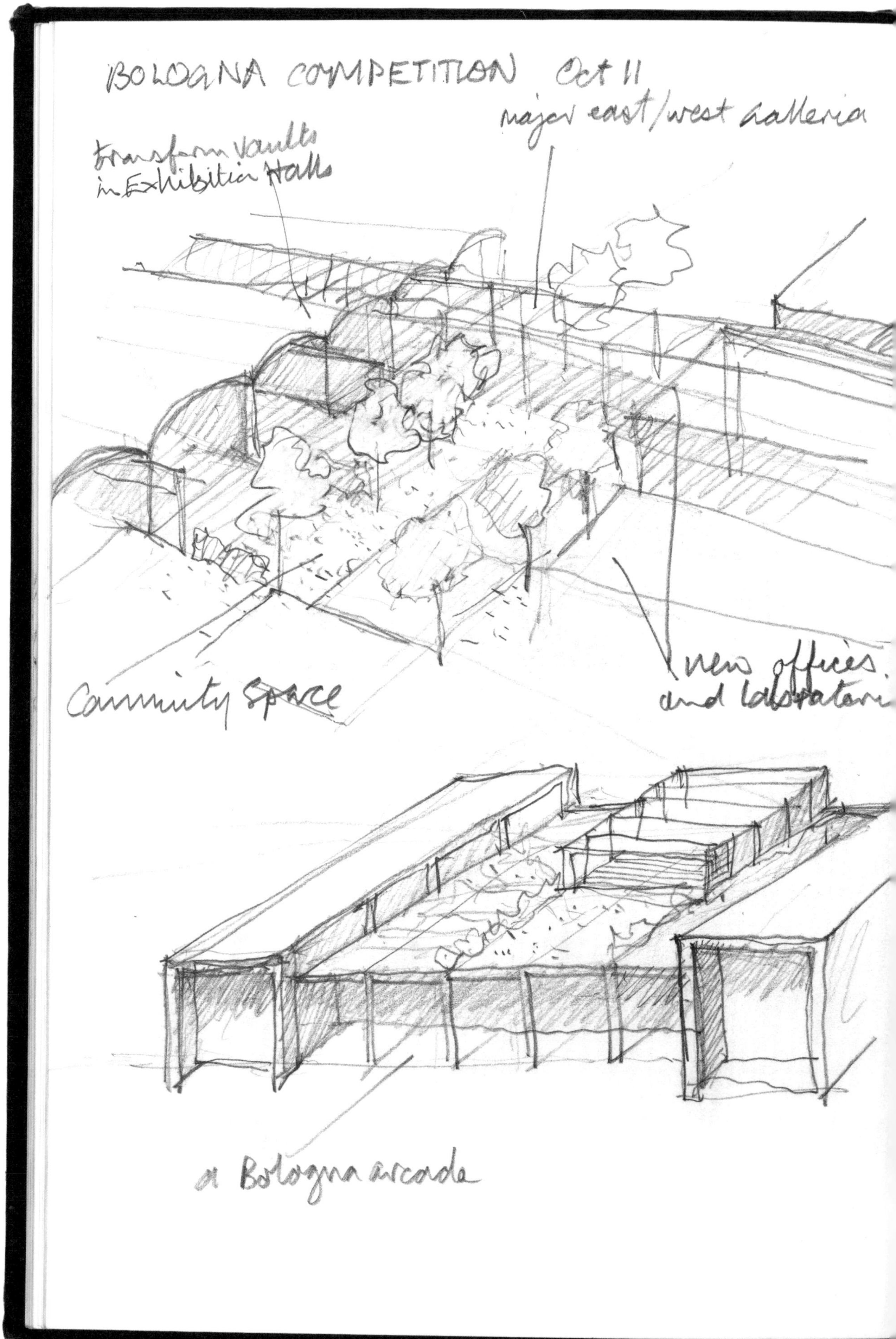

BOLOGNA COMPETITION Oct 11

transform vaults
in Exhibition Halls

major east/west galleria

new offices
and laboratori

Community space

a Bologna arcade

open up the diagrid

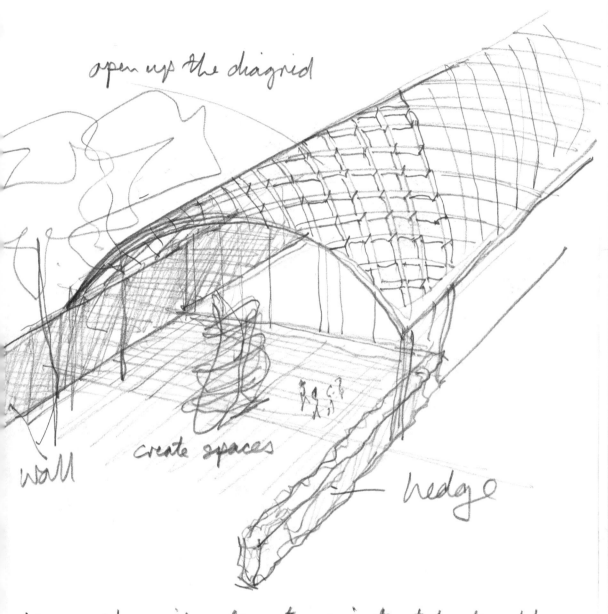

wall

create spaces

hedge

Keep Nervi's structure intact but add new uses.

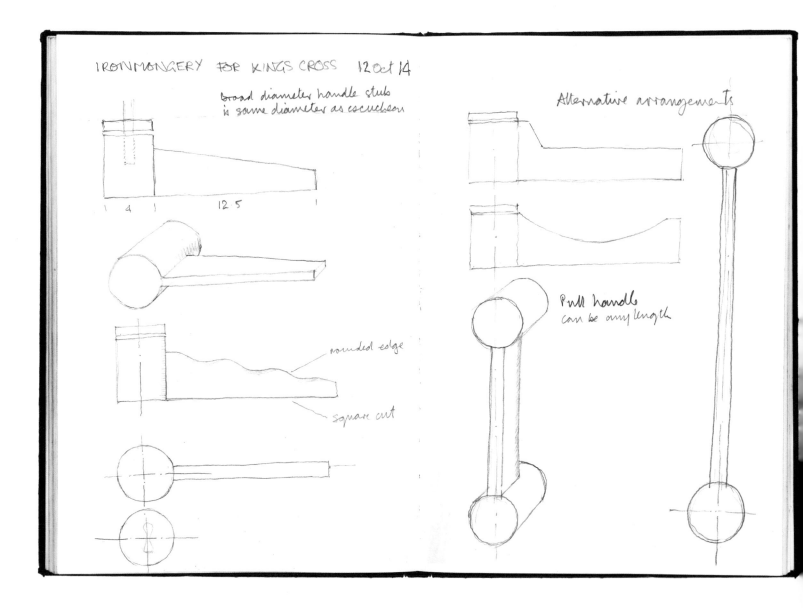

IRONMONGERY FOR KINGS CROSS   12 Oct 14

broad diameter handle stub
is same diameter as escucheon

Alternative arrangements

1 4 1   12 5 1

rounded edge

square cut

Pull handle
can be any length

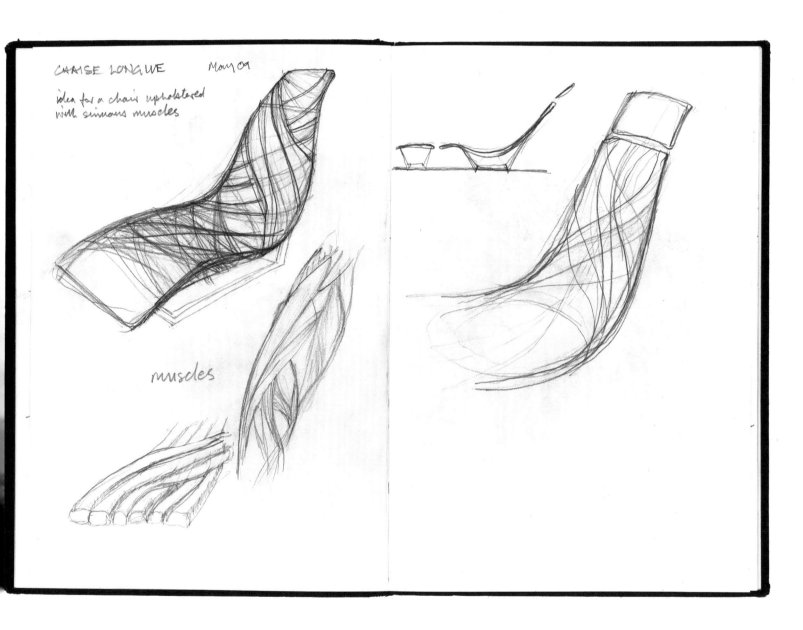

CHAISE LONGUE   May 09

idea for a chair upholstered
with sinuous muscles

muscles

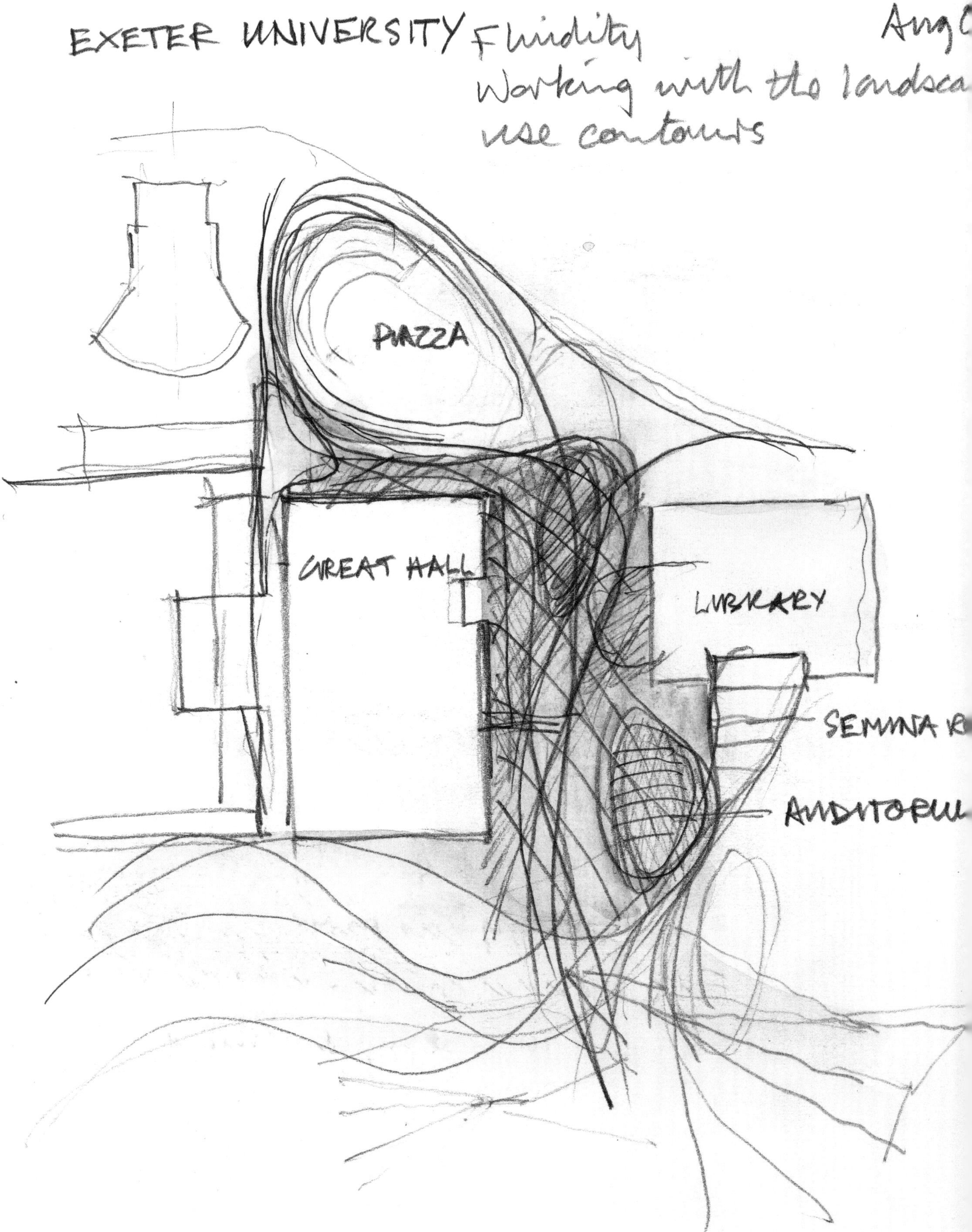

EXETER UNIVERSITY Fluidity
Working with the landsca
use contours

Aug C

PIAZZA

GREAT HALL

LIBRARY

SEMINAR

AUDITORIU

GRIDSHELL ROOF MAKES CONNECTIONS

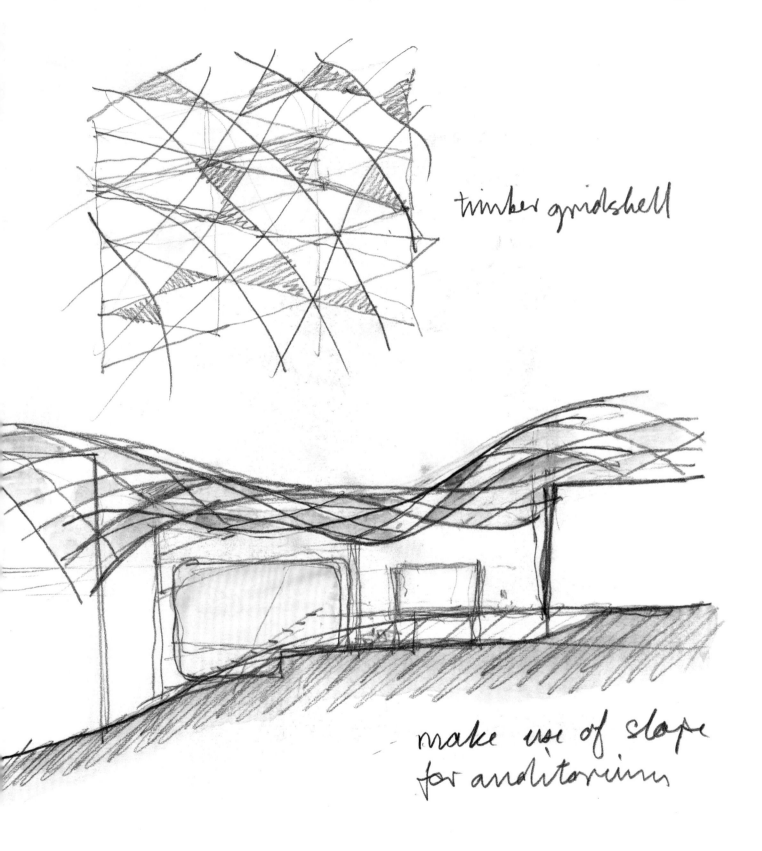

timber gridshell

make use of slope
for auditorium

ISLAMIC CANOPY FOR SHARJAH

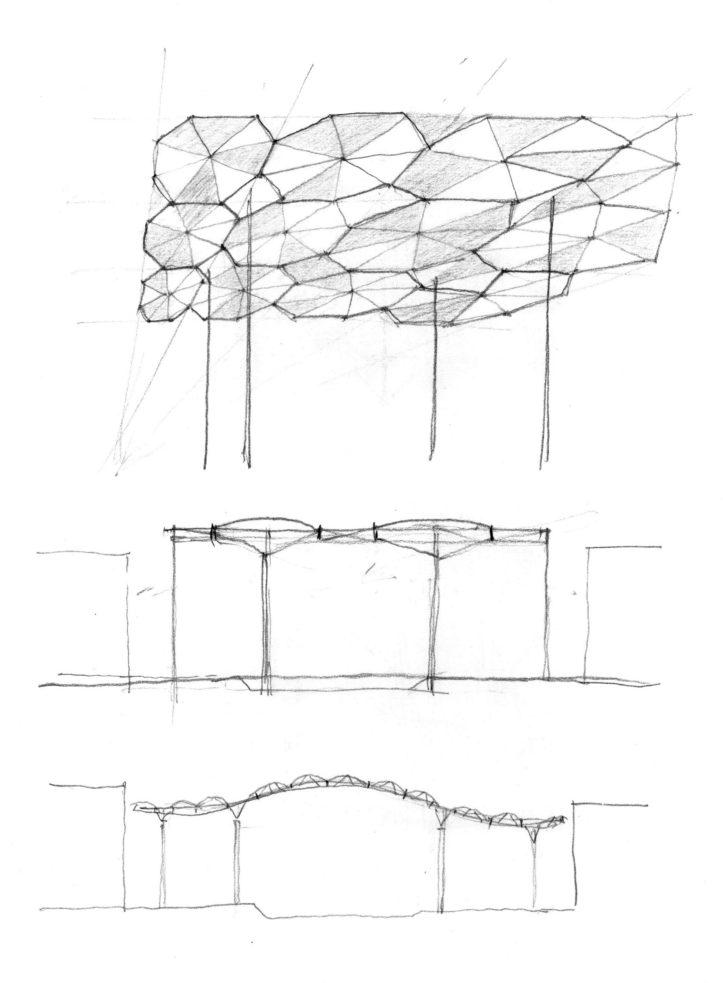

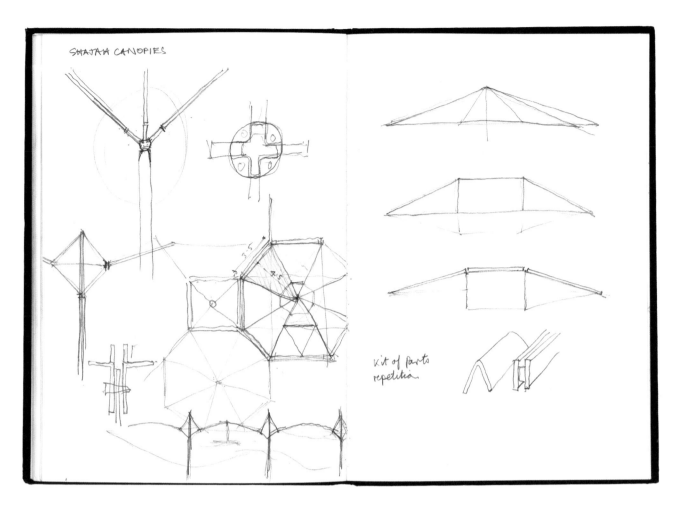

SHAJAH CANOPIES

kit of parts
repetition

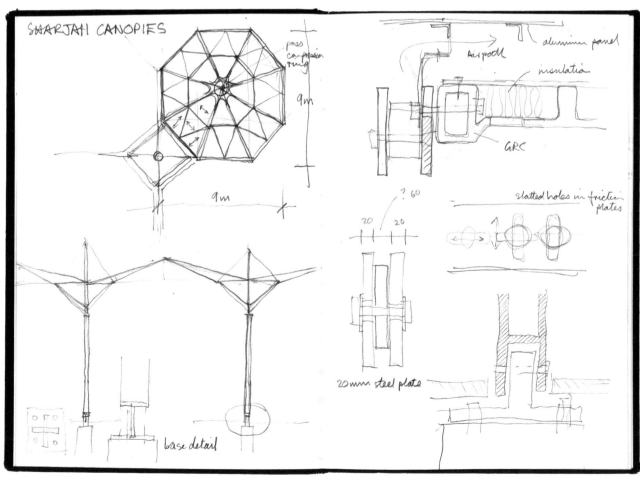

SHARJAH CANOPIES

pass
compression
ring

9m

9m

aluminum panel

Air pool

insulation

GRC

slatted holes in friction
plates

? 60

20 / 20

20mm steel plate

base detail

SALFORD BRIDGE   30 Jan 07
design session with James

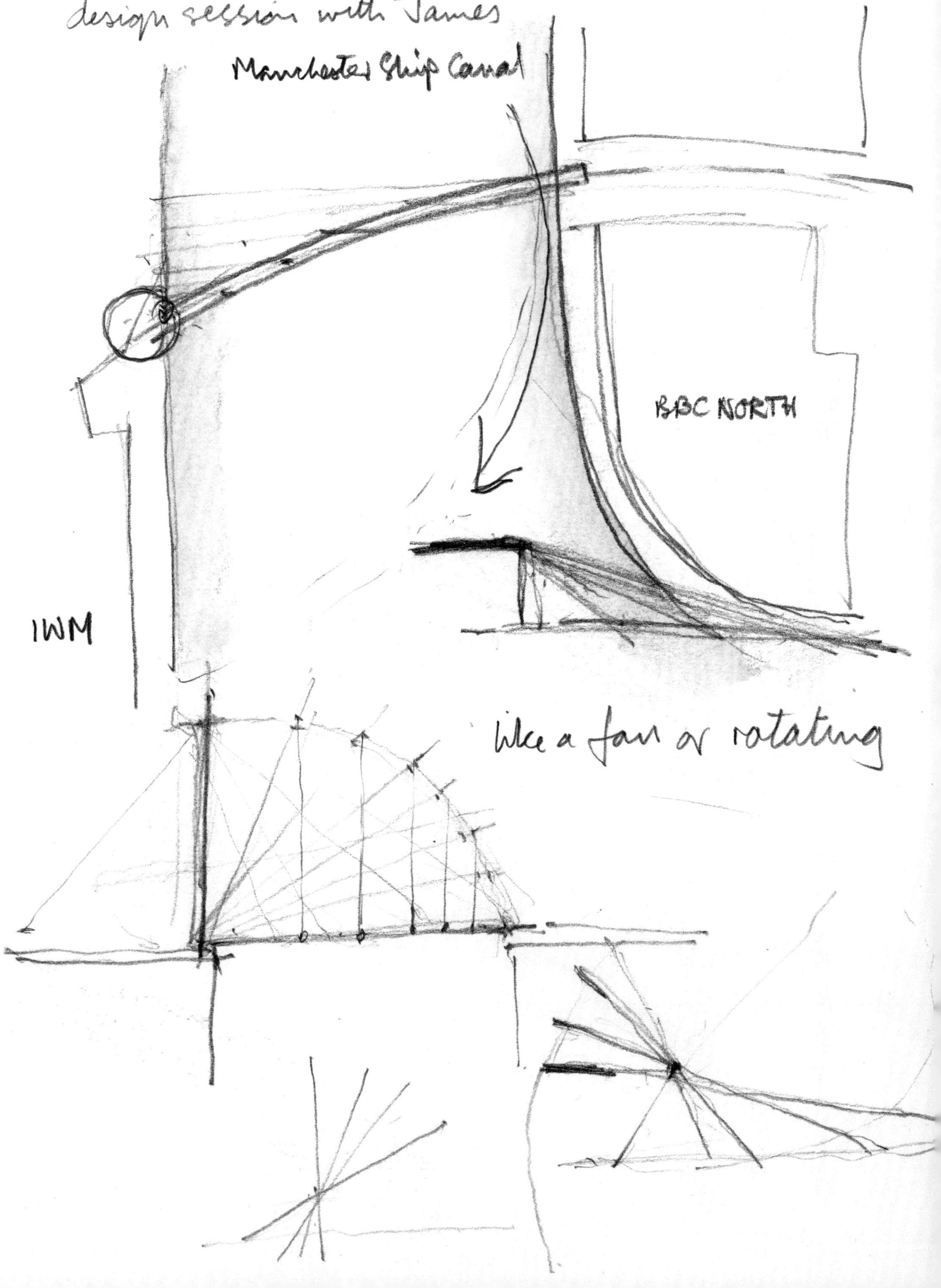

Manchester Ship Canal

BBC NORTH

IWM

like a fan or rotating

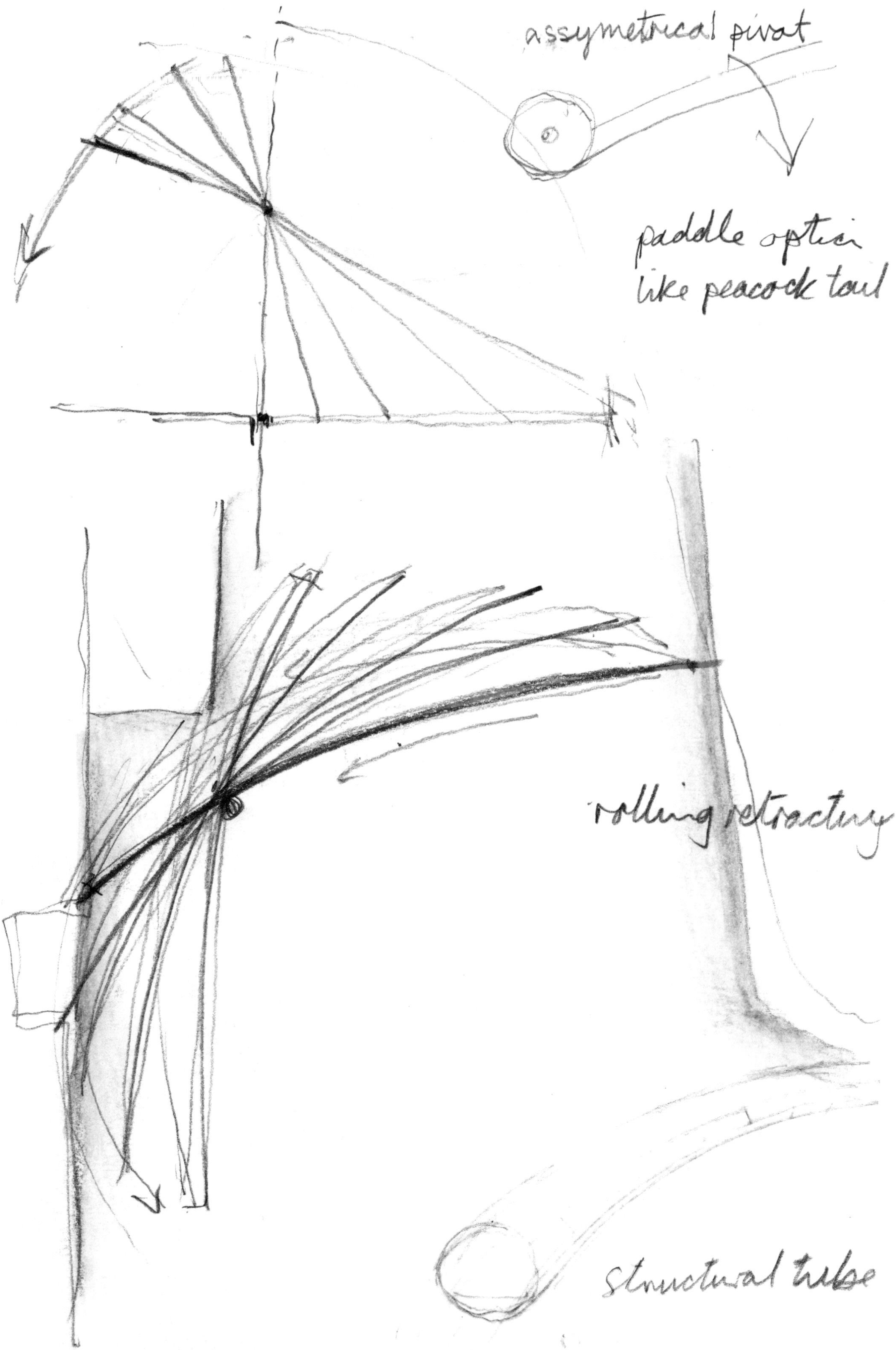

assymetrical pivot

paddle optics
like peacock tail

rolling retractors

structural tube

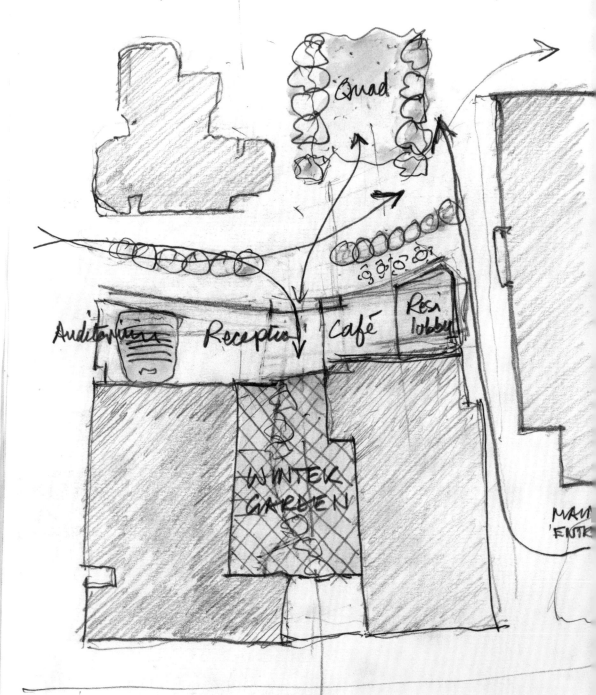

Quad

Auditorium   Reception   Café   Resi lobby

WINTER GARDEN

MAIN ENTR

A single long low building
with stratas of accommodation
in place of two individual buildings

Graduate School 'Identity'

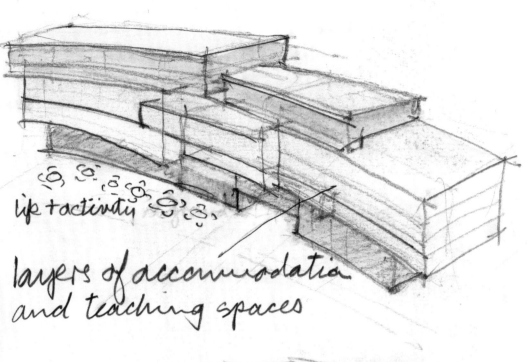

life + activity

layers of accommodation
and teaching spaces

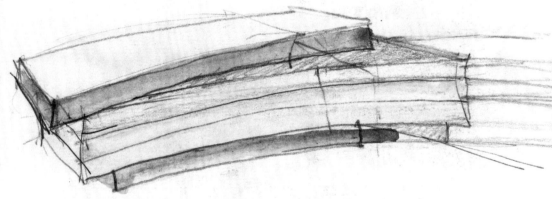

Bridge the Gap + Unify

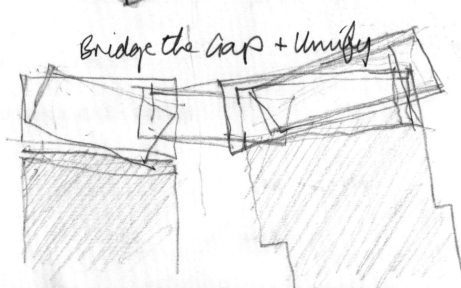

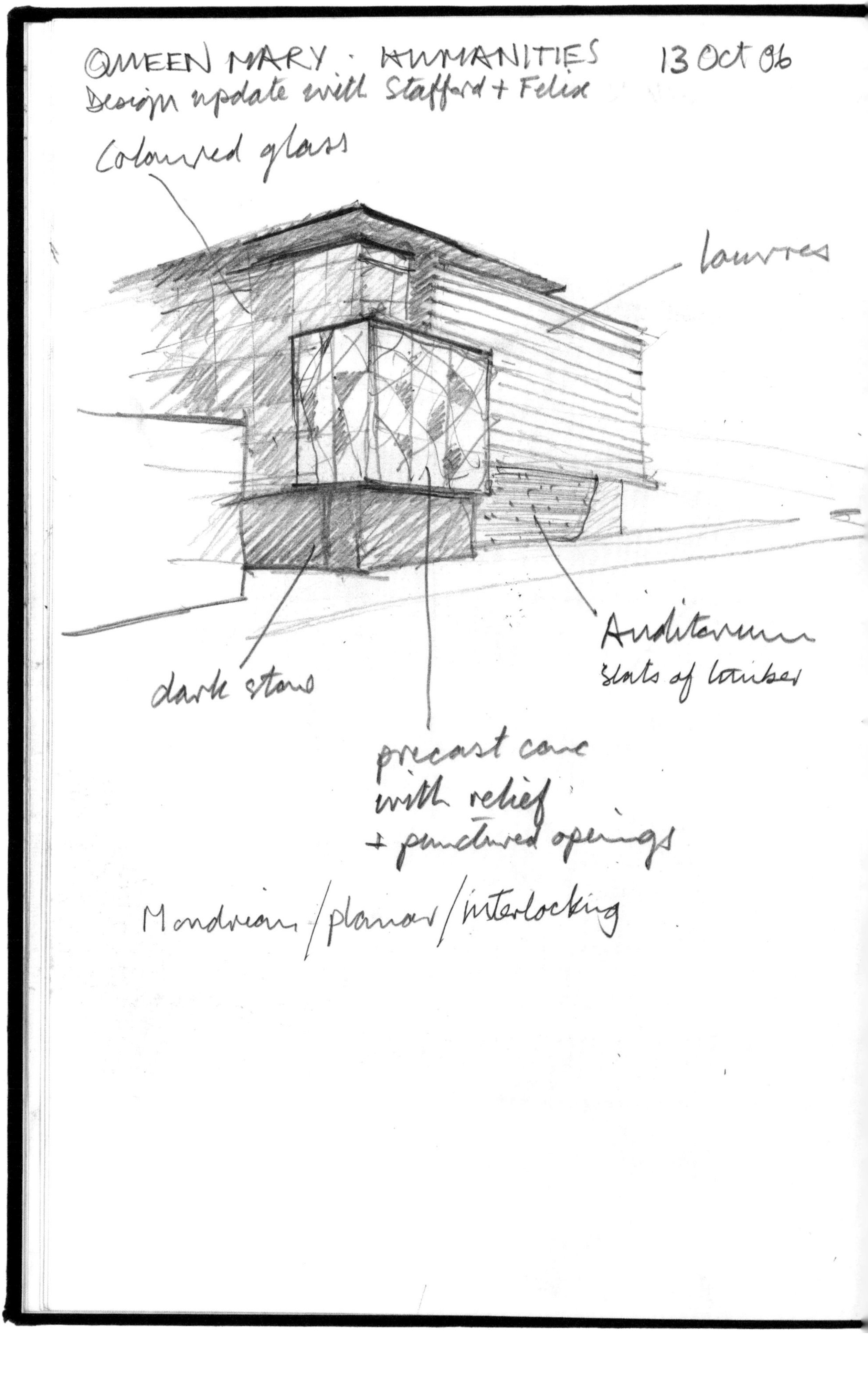

@QUEEN MARY · HUMANITIES   13 Oct 96
Design update with Stafford + Felix

Coloured glass

louvres

dark stone

Auditorium
slats of timber

precast cone
with relief
+ punctured openings

Mondrian / planar / interlocking

colour OPTIONS to create strong impact on Mile End Rd

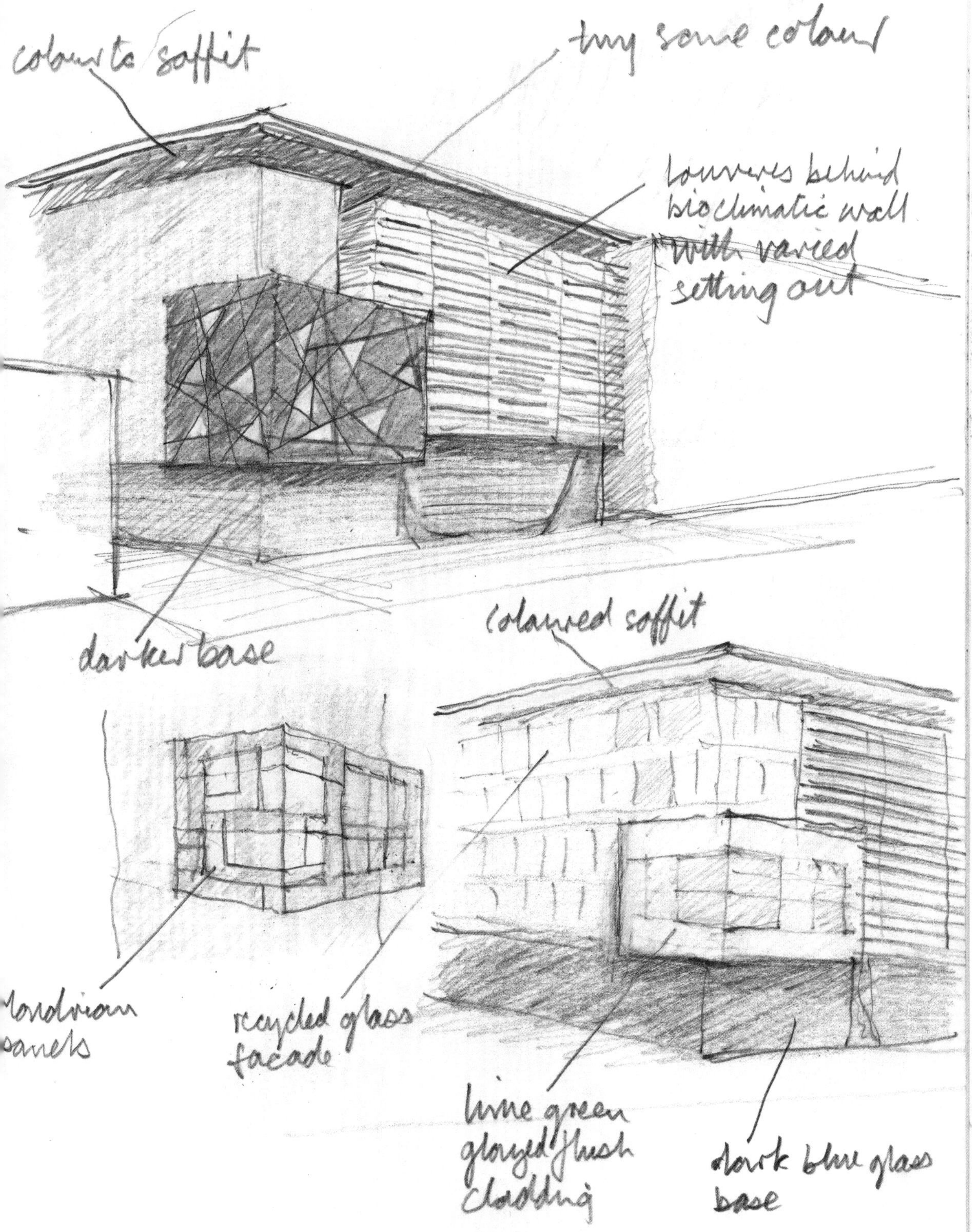

colour to soffit

try same colour

louvres behind
bioclimatic wall
with varied
setting out

darker base

coloured soffit

Mondrian
panels

recycled glass
facade

lime green
glazed flush
cladding

dark blue glass
base

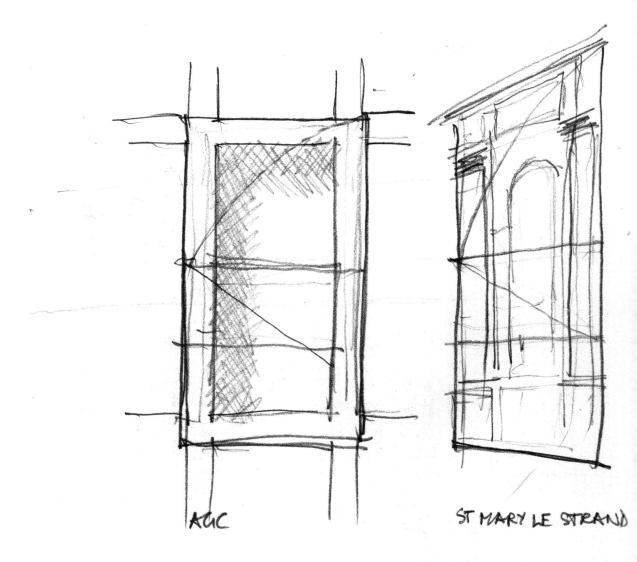

AGC

ST MARY LE STRAND

SAME PROPORTIONS
Diagram for AGC Public Inquiry

GOLDEN SECTION

MANSARD ROOF

ST MARY'S LE STRAND

THE STRAND

ARUNDEL GREAT COURT   Sketch at Public Inquiry

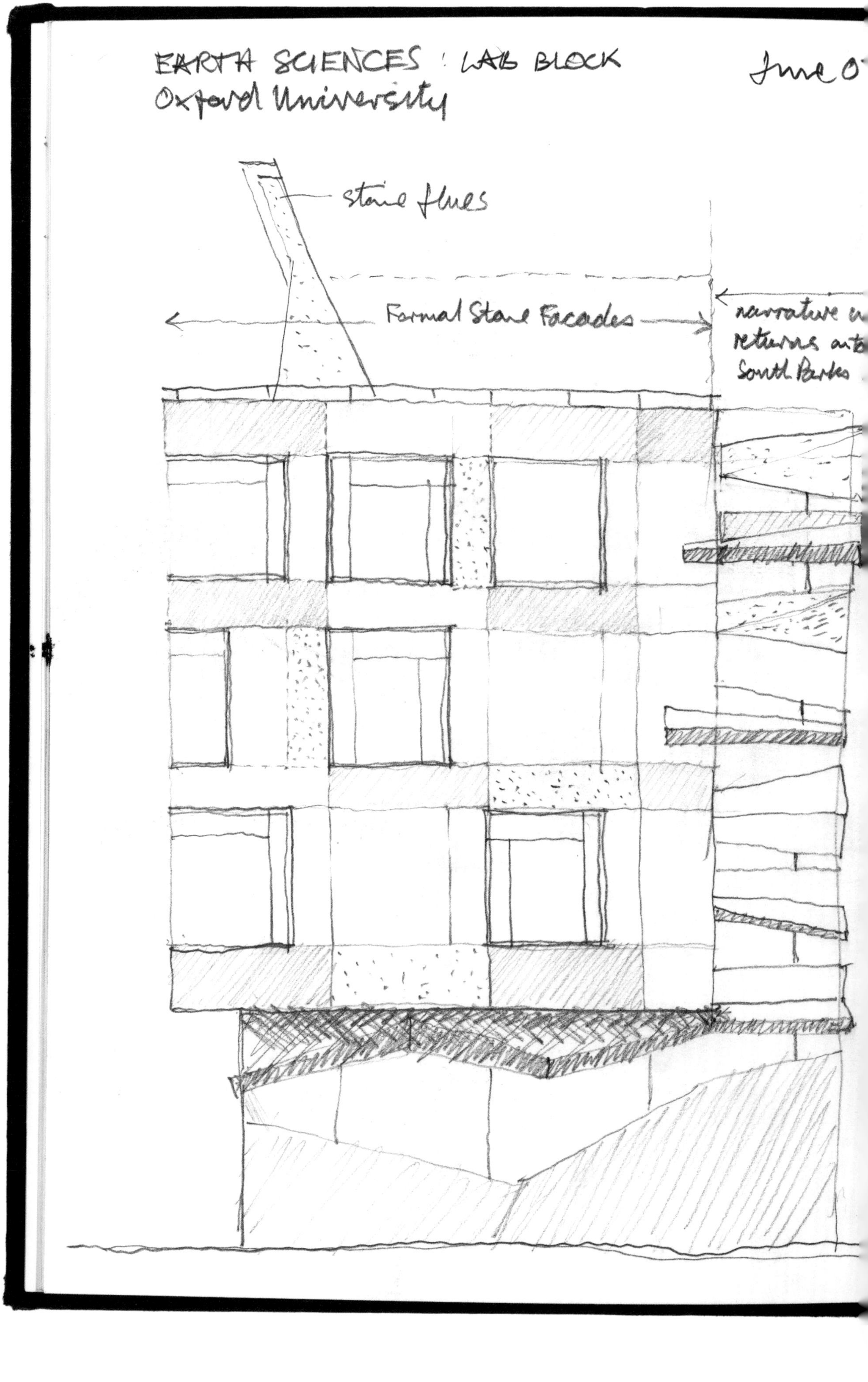

EARTH SCIENCES : LAB BLOCK
Oxford University

June 0

stone flues

← Formal Stone Facades →

← narrative w
returns ant
South Parks

Narrative wall takes the form of rock strata
with angled surfaces

2 different stones in strata with layer of translucent stone
and layers of glass

July 02

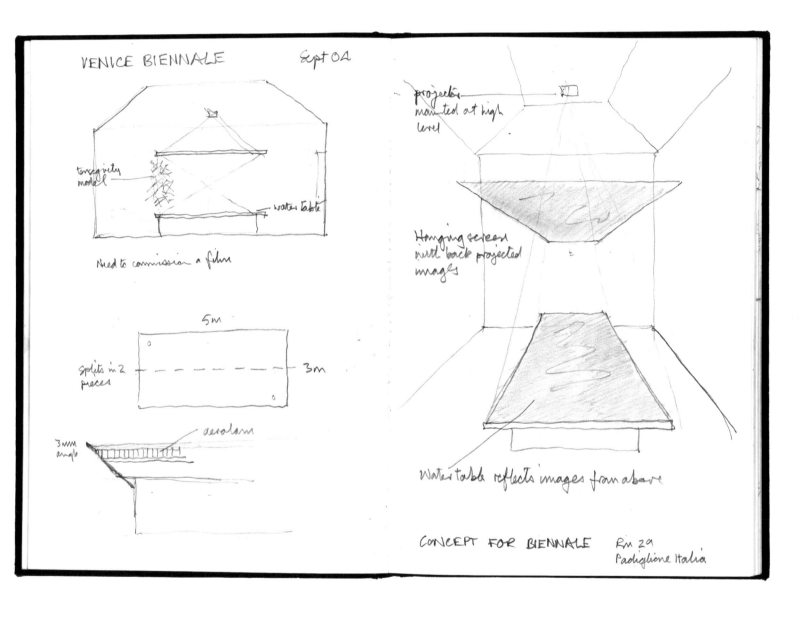

VENICE BIENNALE   Sept 04

tensegrity model

water table

Need to commission a film

5m

Splits in 2 pieces

3m

aerolam

3mm angle

projector mounted at high level

Hanging screen with back projected images

Water table reflects images from above

CONCEPT FOR BIENNALE   Rm 29
Padiglione Italia

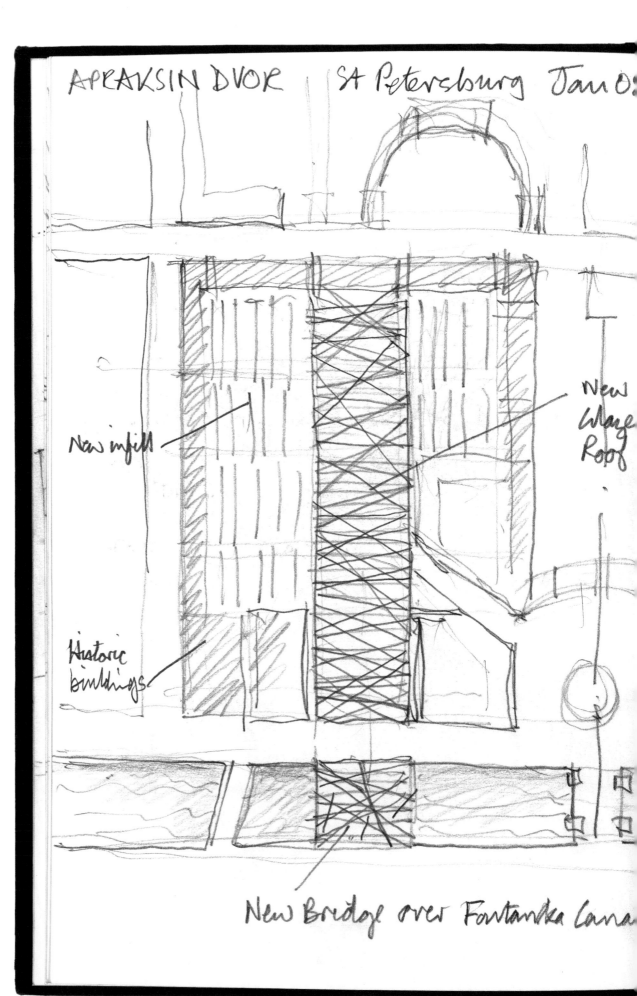

New infill

New
Wave
Roof

Historic
buildings

New Bridge over Fontanka Canal

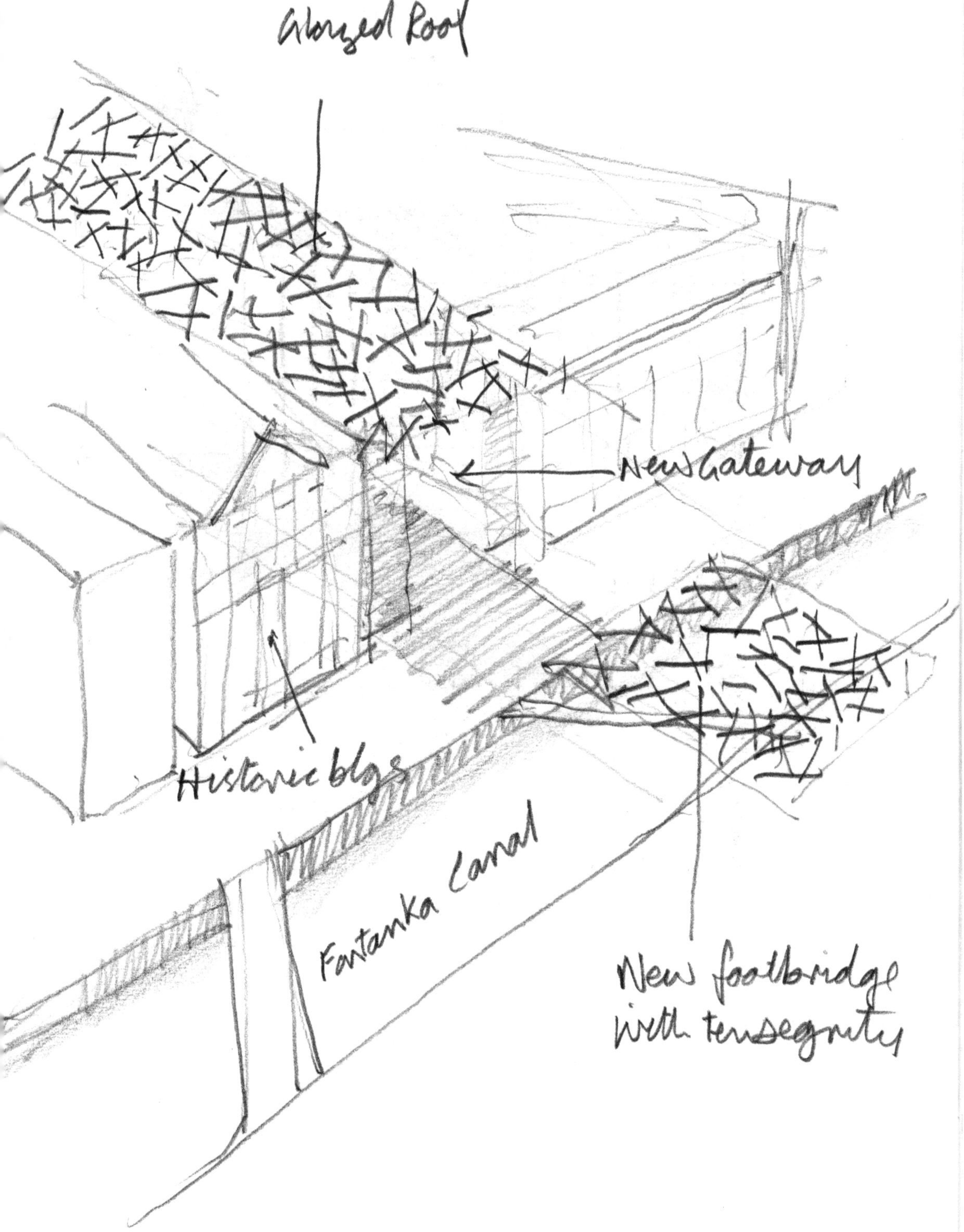

Glazed Roof

New Gateway

Historic blgs

Fontanka Canal

New footbridge
with tensegrity

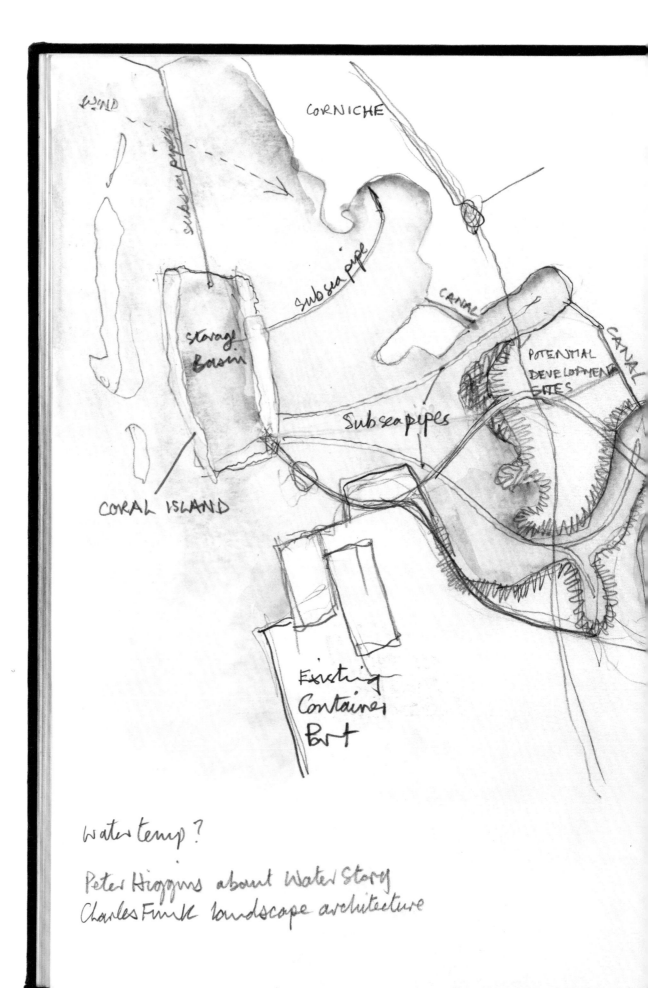

WIND

CORNICHE

subsea pipe

subsea pipe

CANAL

CANAL

storage Basin

POTENTIAL DEVELOPMENT SITES

Subsea pipes

CORAL ISLAND

Existing Container Port

water temp?

Peter Higgins about water story
Charles Funk landscape architecture

A basin of 1 Km² water is
created between two dead
coral reefs. When the tide
comes in, the pressure forces
the water from the basin
down subsea pipes to
flush out the lagoons
bringing life back to
the city and the
potential for new development

Strategy Plan
Diagrams
Narrative
Zoning — uses
        — densities
Identity + characters

Show the grain of
            development
Environmental aspects
3D contour for devel

JEDDAH
Roofscape / Landscape

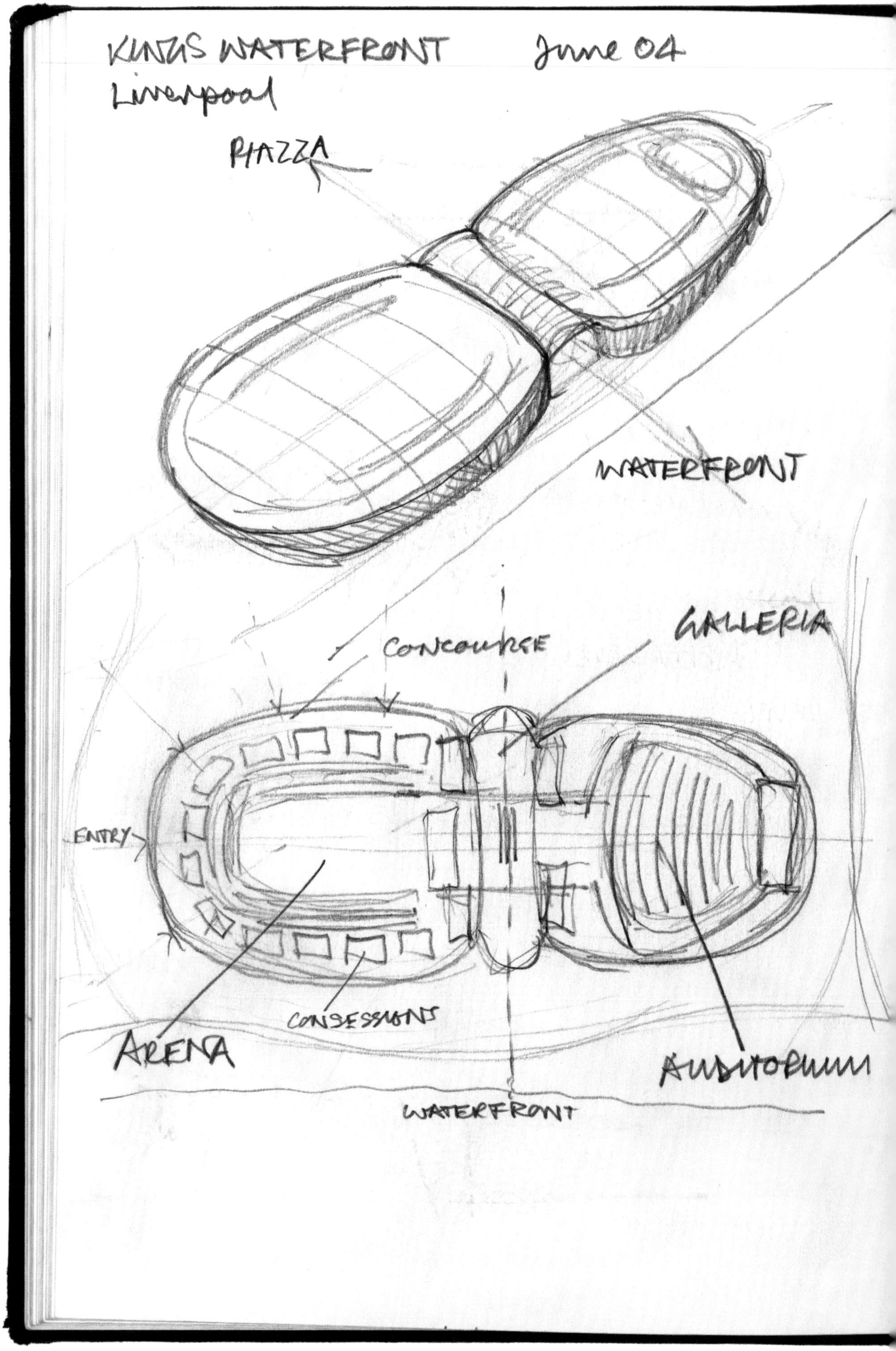

KINGS WATERFRONT   June 04
Liverpool

PIAZZA

WATERFRONT

CONCOURSE   GALLERIA

ENTRY

CONSESSIONS

ARENA

AUDITORIUM

WATERFRONT

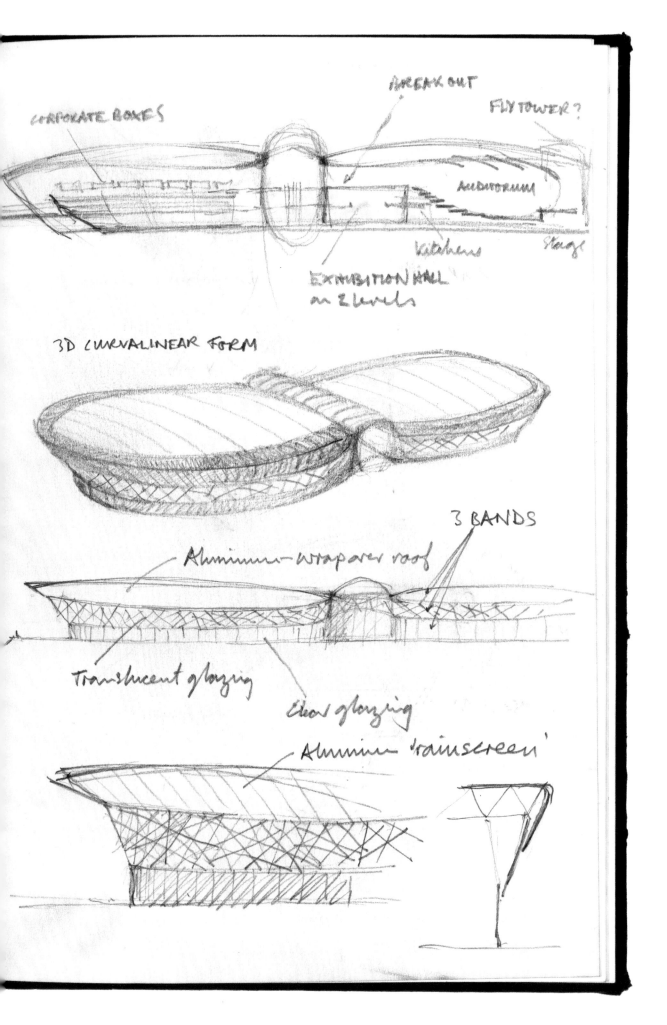

CORPORATE BOXES

BREAK OUT

FLY TOWER?

AUDITORIUM

Kitchens

Stage

EXHIBITION HALL
on 2 levels

3D CURVALINEAR FORM

3 BANDS

Aluminium wrapover roof

Translucent glazing

Clear glazing

Aluminium 'rainscreen'

KINGS CLADDING DETAIL 13 Jan 06

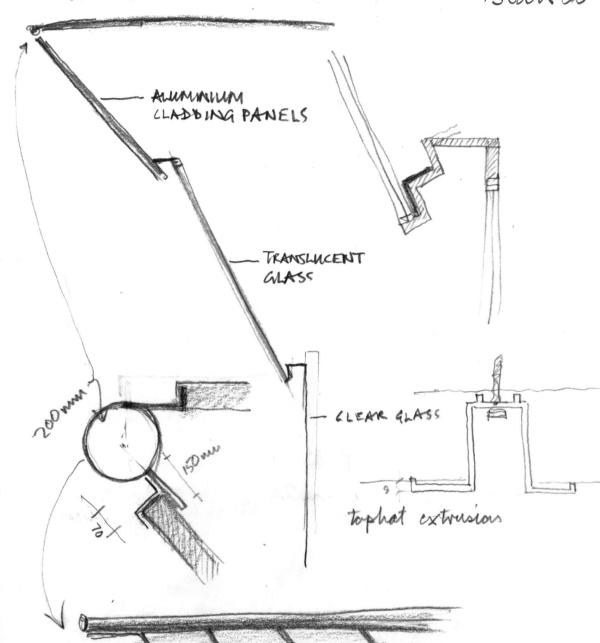

ALUMINIUM
CLADDING PANELS

TRANSLUCENT
GLASS

200mm

150mm

70

CLEAR GLASS

tophat extrusion

Review with Stephan, Olly + Eric + Ivan

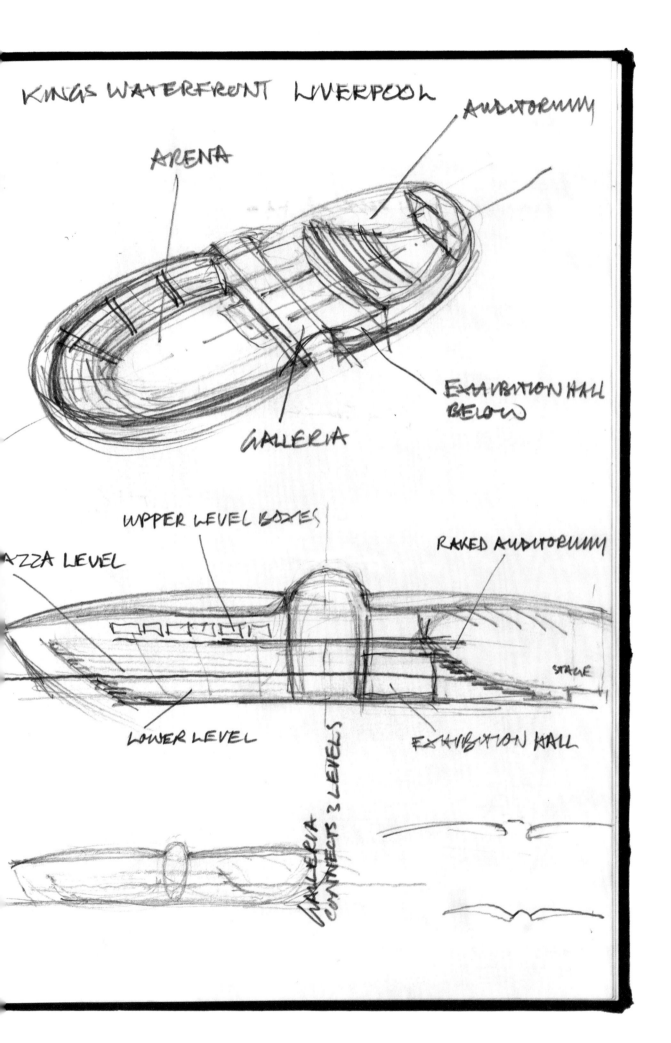

KINGS WATERFRONT LIVERPOOL

ARENA

AUDITORIUM

GALLERIA

EXHIBITION HALL BELOW

UPPER LEVEL BOXES

PIAZZA LEVEL

RAKED AUDITORIUM

STAGE

LOWER LEVEL

GALLERIA CONNECTS 3 LEVELS

EXHIBITION HALL

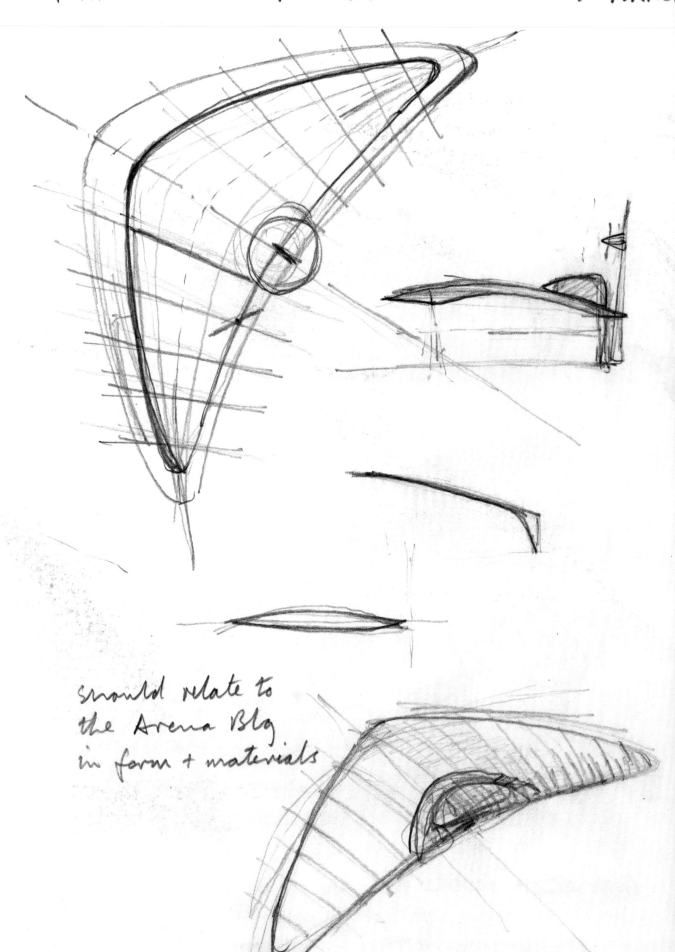

PAVILION ON KINGS WATERFRONT   30 MARCH

should relate to
the Arena Blg
in form + materials

Aluminum rainscreen

Glazed wall

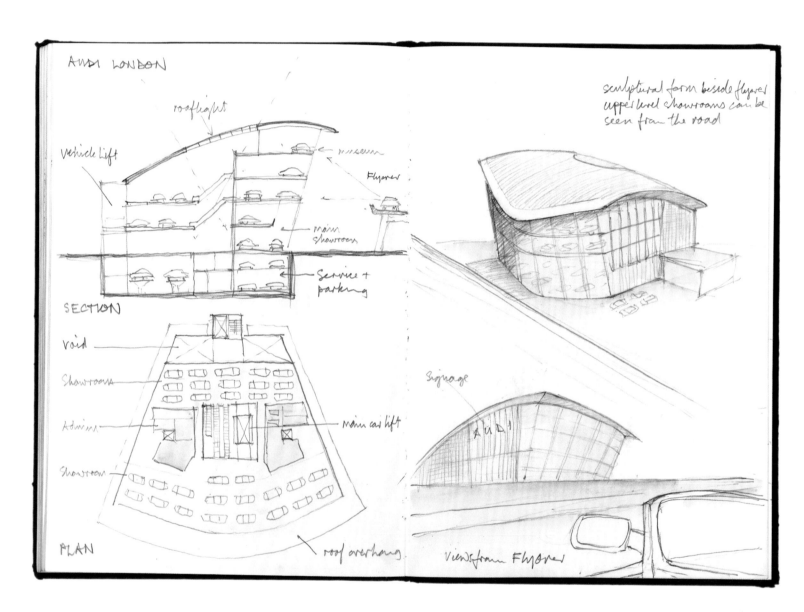

AUDI LONDON

sculptural form beside flyover
upper level showrooms can be
seen from the road

roofflight

vehicle lift

museum

Flyover

main
showroom

Service +
parking

SECTION

void

Showrooms

Admins

main car lift

Showroom

PLAN

roof overhang

Signage

AUDI

views from Flyover

AUDI COMPETITION
Regional HQ Glasgow

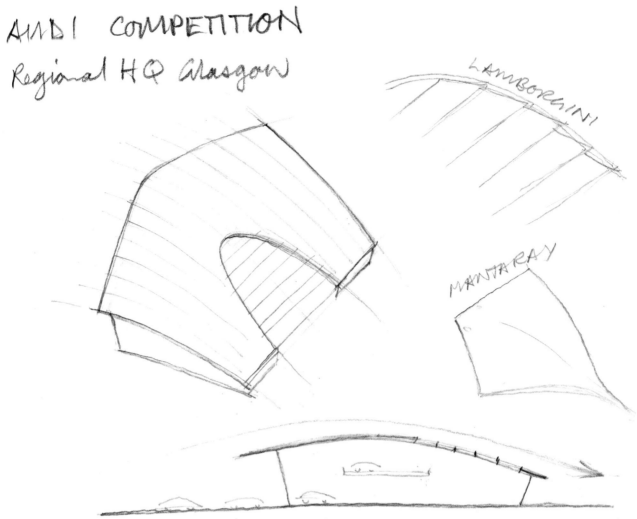

LAMBORGHINI

MANTARAY

Flat curves sleek aerodynamic

AUDI

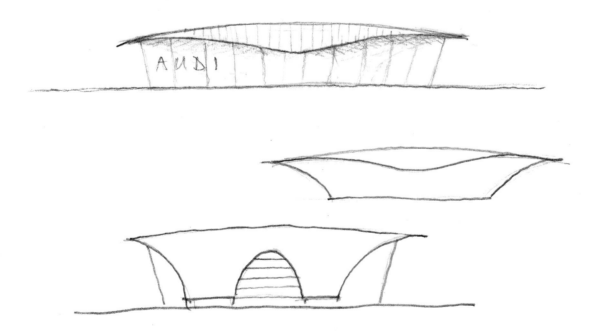

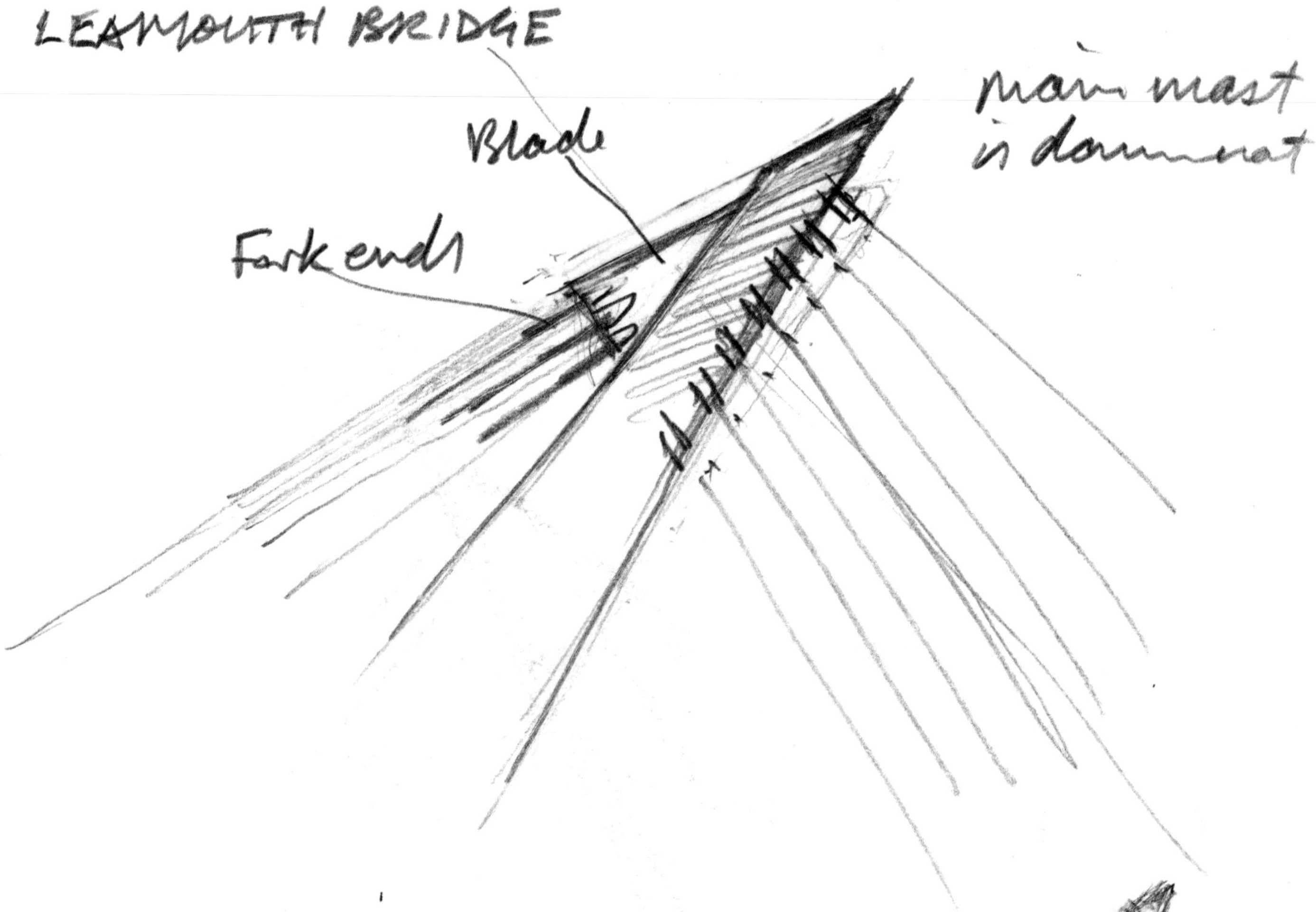

LEAMOUTH BRIDGE

Blade

Fork ends

main mast
is dominant

WEAMOUTH BRIDGE

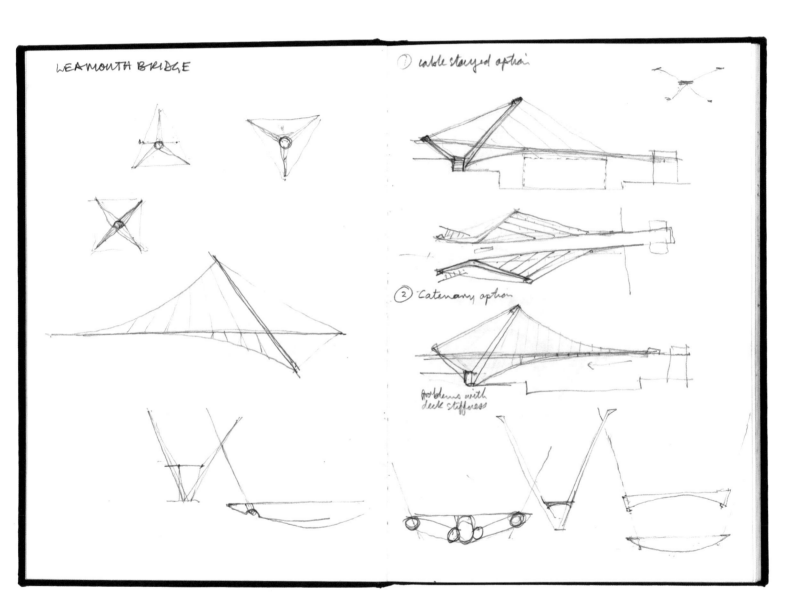

① cable stayed option

② catenary option

Problems with
deck stiffness

AMNESTY

Algorythmic Script

2 no   5m × 2·5m   with 75mm × 75 pixels
welded polythene sheet for the display
can also be embeded into the blg.

Pavilion in the pa
GRC preast pane
provide a screen
around a glass b

Complex 3D curvalinear facade gives strong visual identity
and helps to create a 'DESTINATION' in Milan

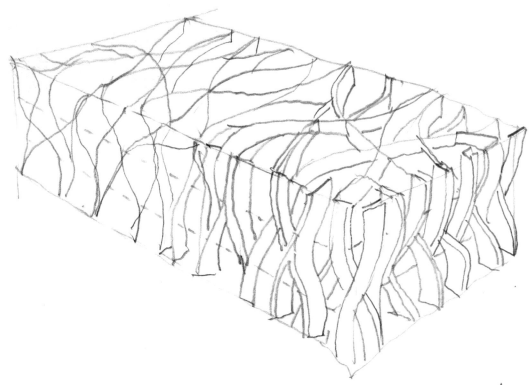

Feb 07

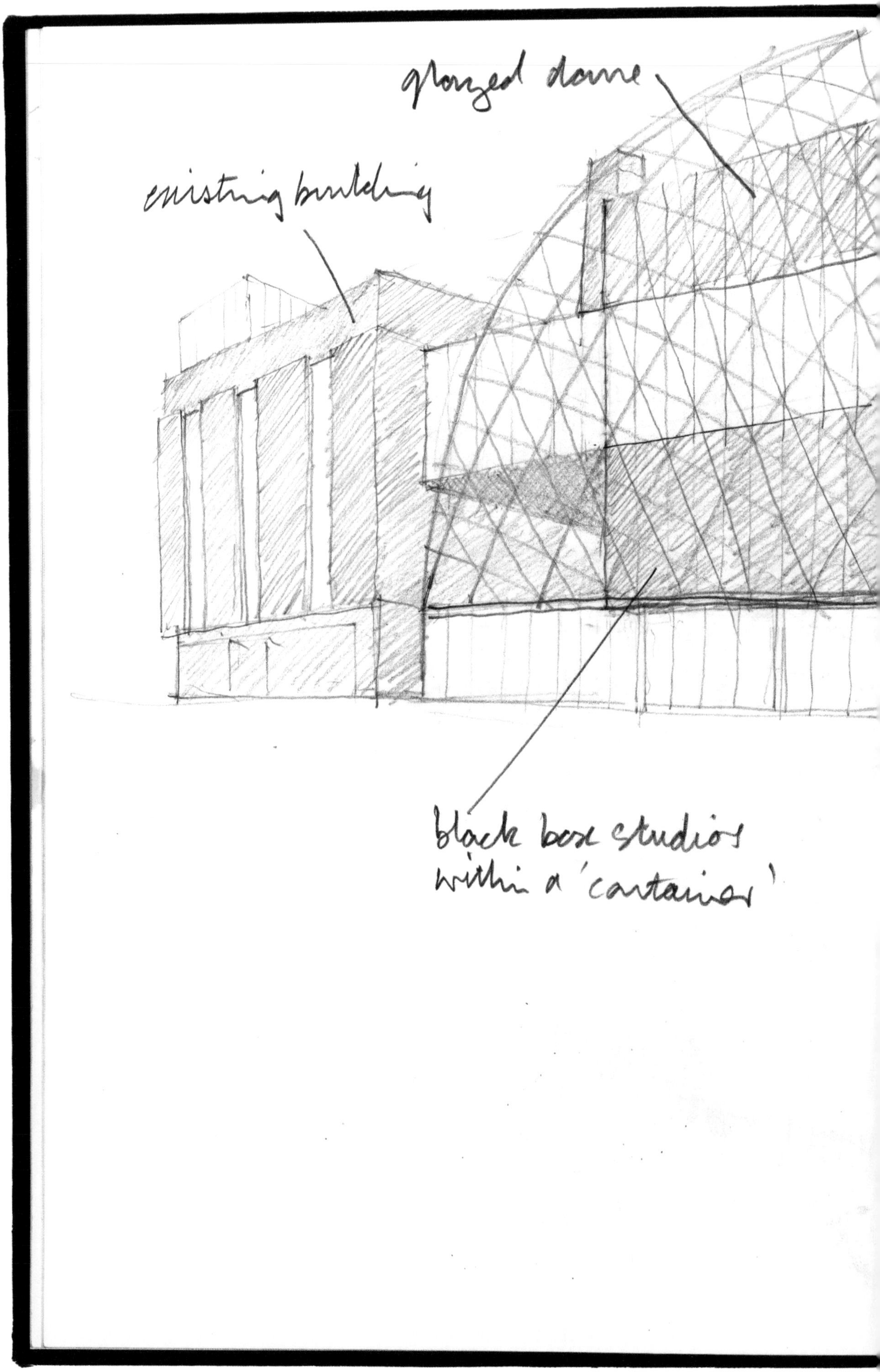

glazed dome

existing building

black box studios
within a 'container'

Competition Board 4
'Breaking Free'

'light box'

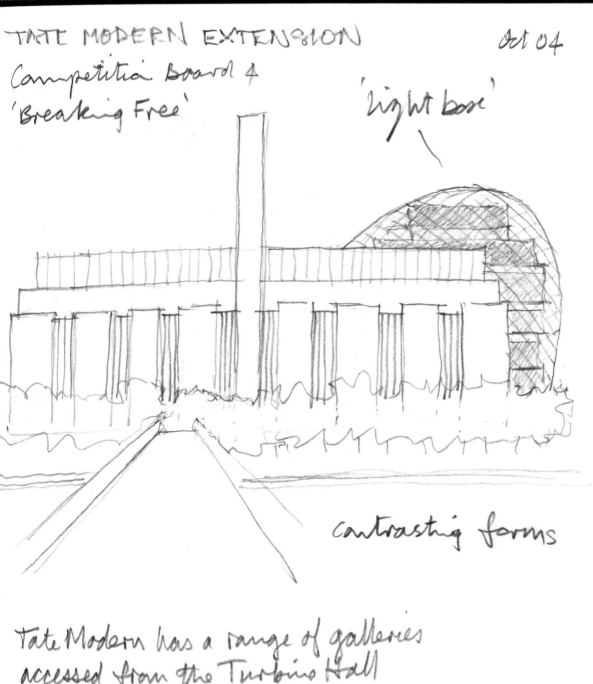

Contrasting forms

Tate Modern has a range of galleries
accessed from the Turbino Hall

A new glazed dome structure
provides an environmental enclosure
in which galleries are constructed
with flexibility to change and adapt.

Edinburgh Botanic Gdns   June 03

- value of biodiversity
- threat to biodiversity
- Role of RBG

'growth'

poetic gesture
to the site + subject
expression of the
meaning

Building as a landscape
living wall

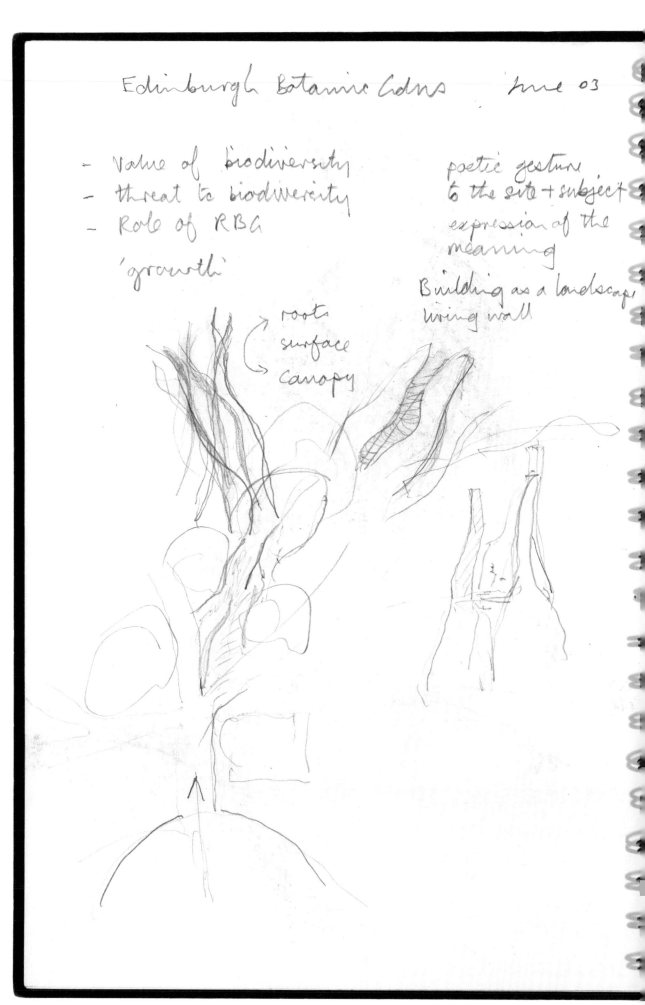

roots
surface
canopy

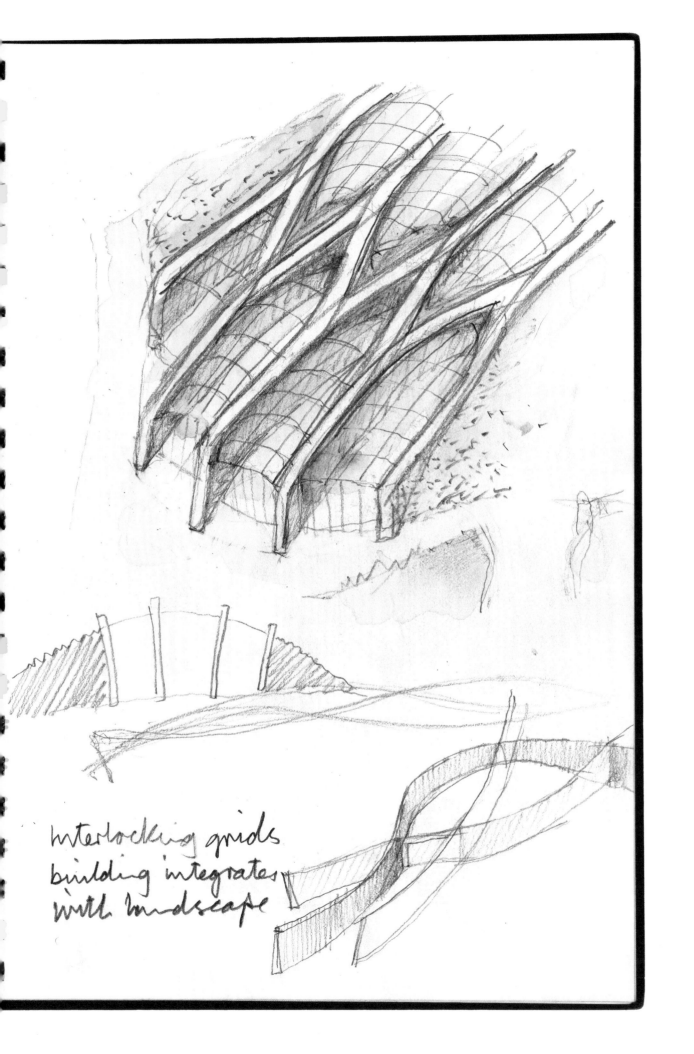

interlocking grids
building integrates
with landscape

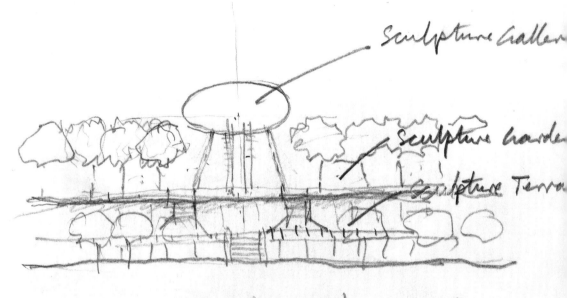

Sculpture Gallery

Sculpture Garden

Sculpture Terrace

Warped Gallery 'floats' over the
sculpture garden on the site of the
Crystal Palace 'Transverse Aisle'

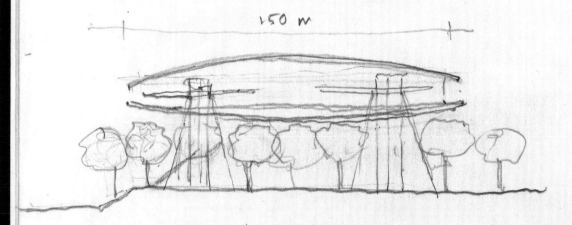

150 m

Design proposal for the Crystal Palace site

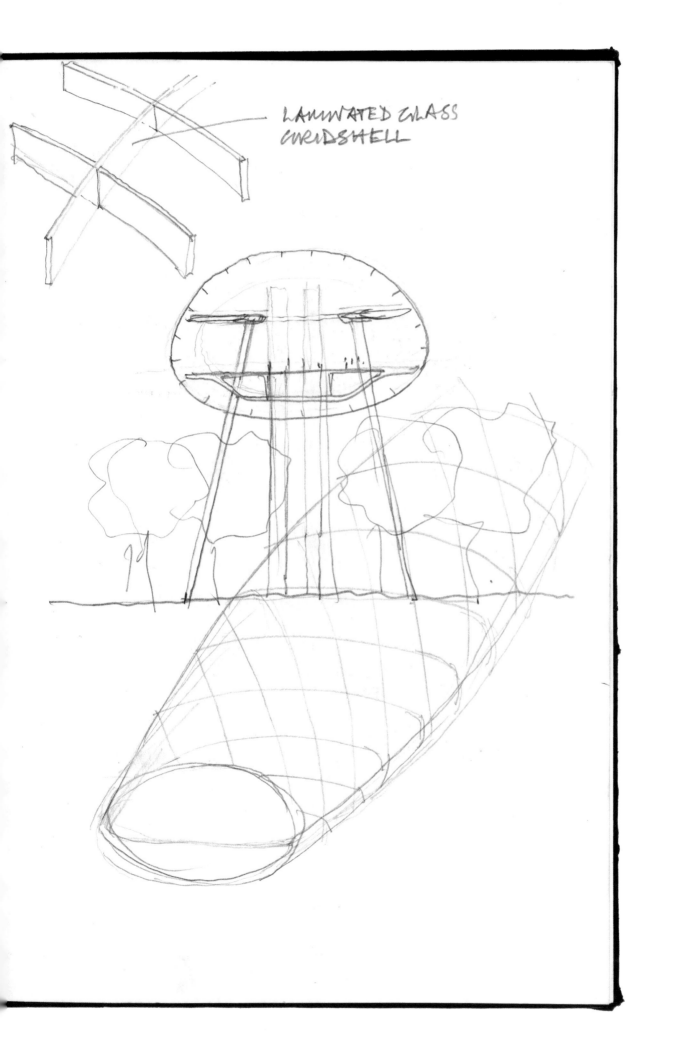

LAMINATED GLASS
GRIDSHELL

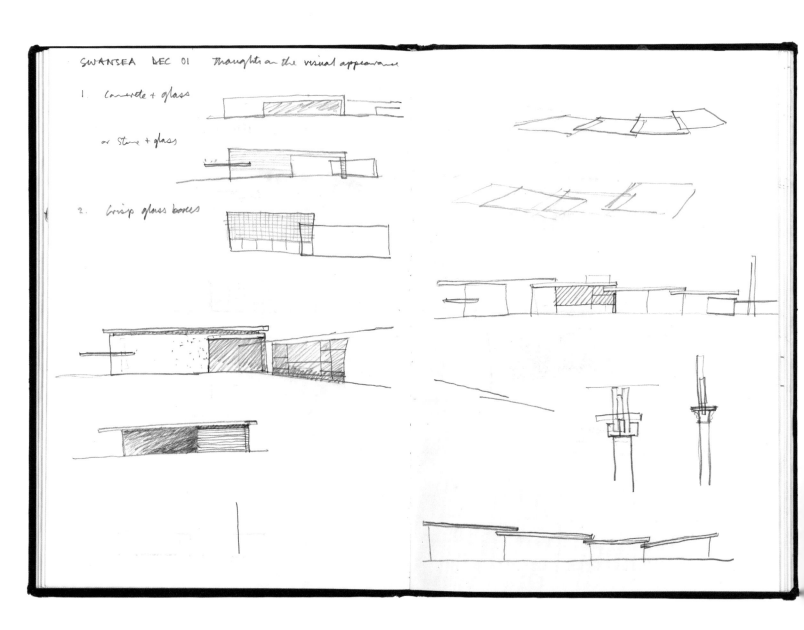

SWANSEA DEC 01   Thoughts on the visual appearance

1. Concrete + glass

   or Stone + glass

2. Crisp glass boxes

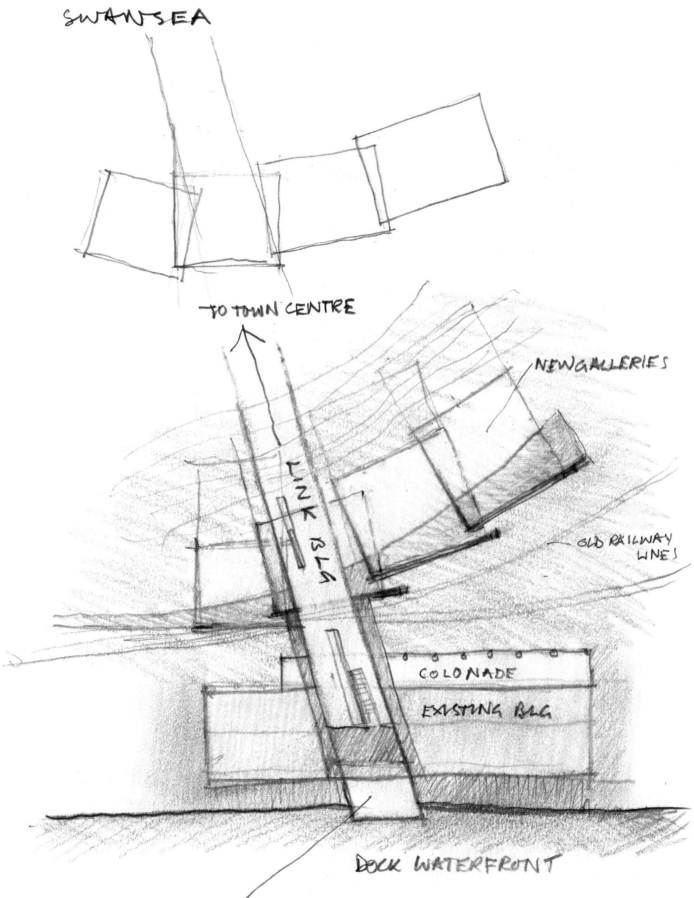

SWANSEA

TO TOWN CENTRE

NEW GALLERIES

LINK BLG

OLD RAILWAY LINES

COLONADE

EXISTING BLG

DOCK WATERFRONT

OVERHANGING CANOPY
catches the reflections

SLATE WALL

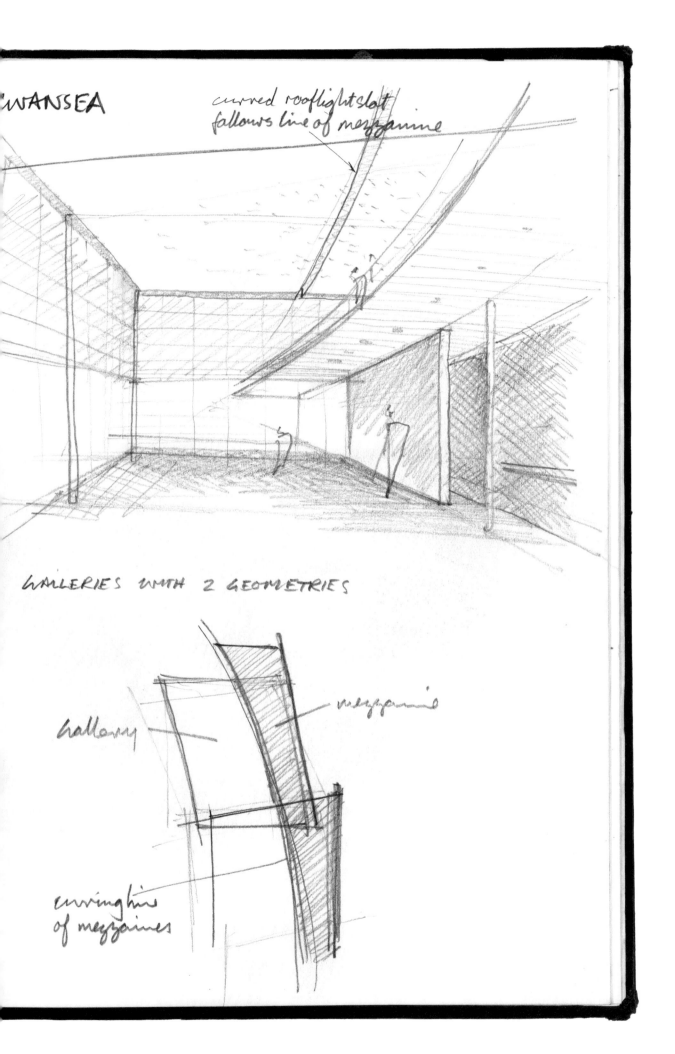

SWANSEA

curved rooflight slot
follows line of mezzanine

GALLERIES WITH 2 GEOMETRIES

gallery

mezzanine

curving line
of mezzanines

DYSON CANOPY   Design Session with Tony

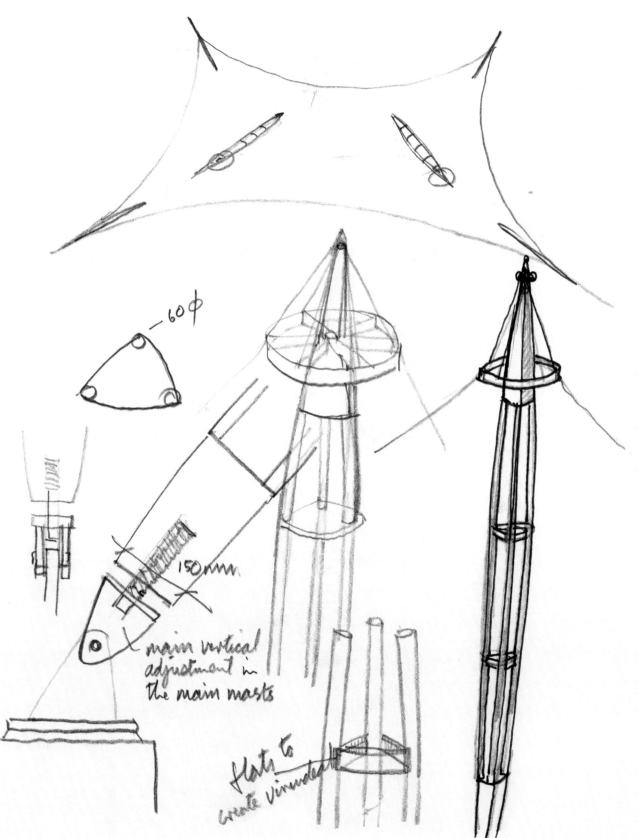

~60φ

150mm

main vertical
adjustment in
the main masts

flats to
create virada

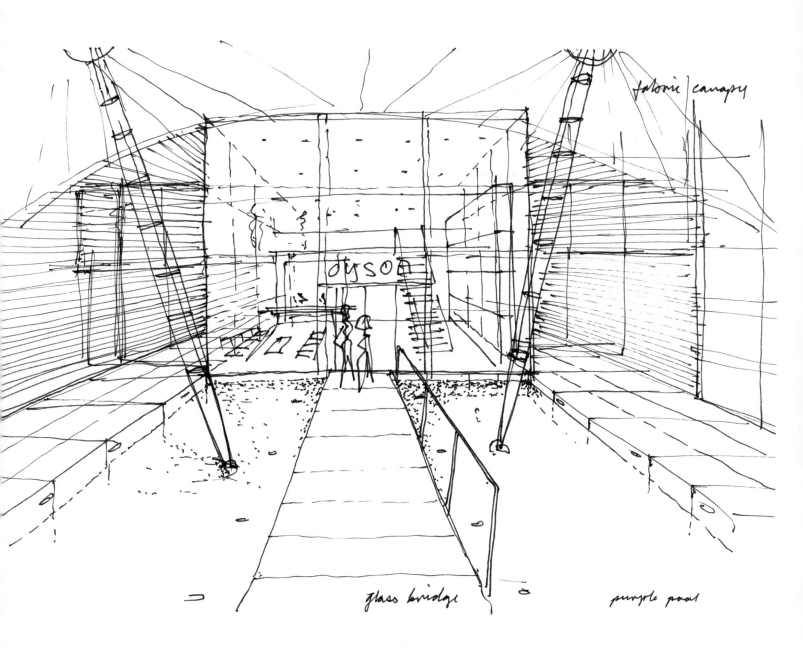

fabric canopy

dyson

glass bridge   purple pool

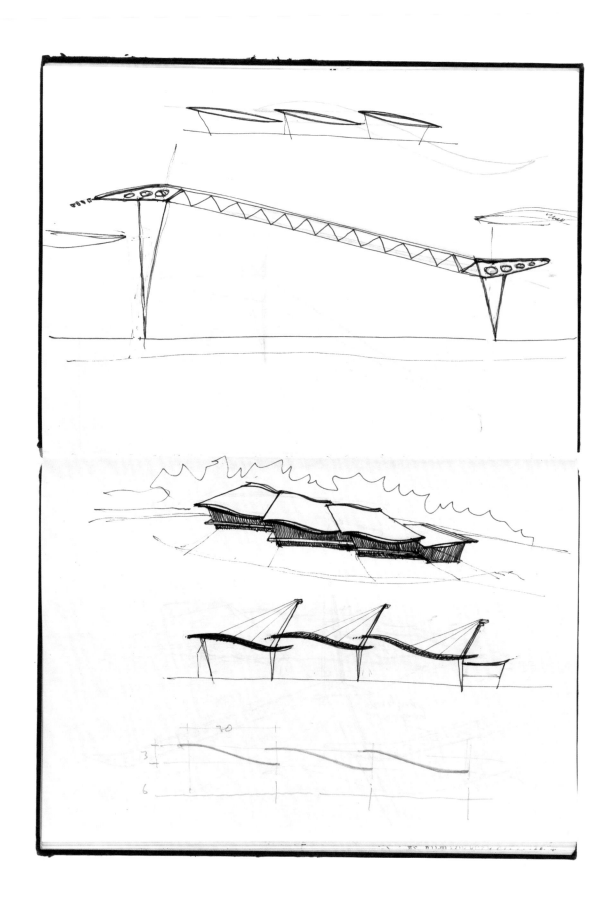

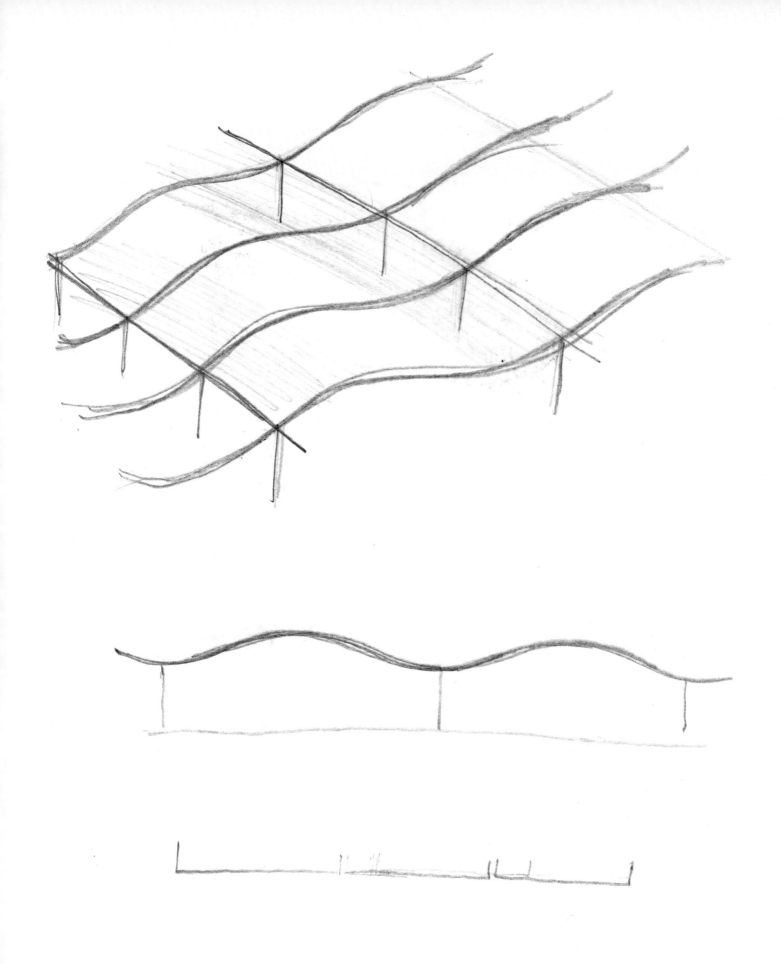

DYSON FACTORY at Malmesbury

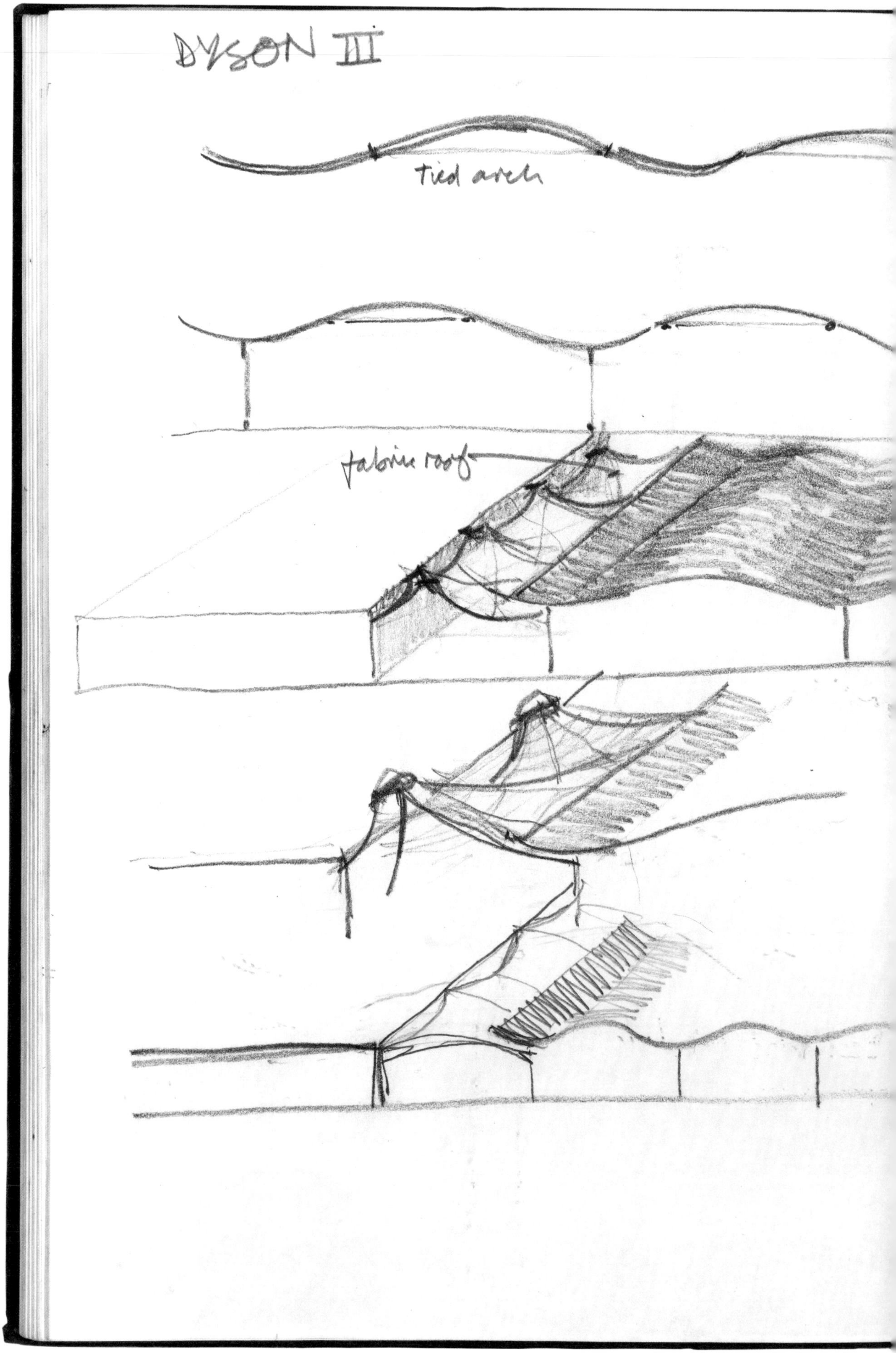

DYSON III

tied arch

fabric roof

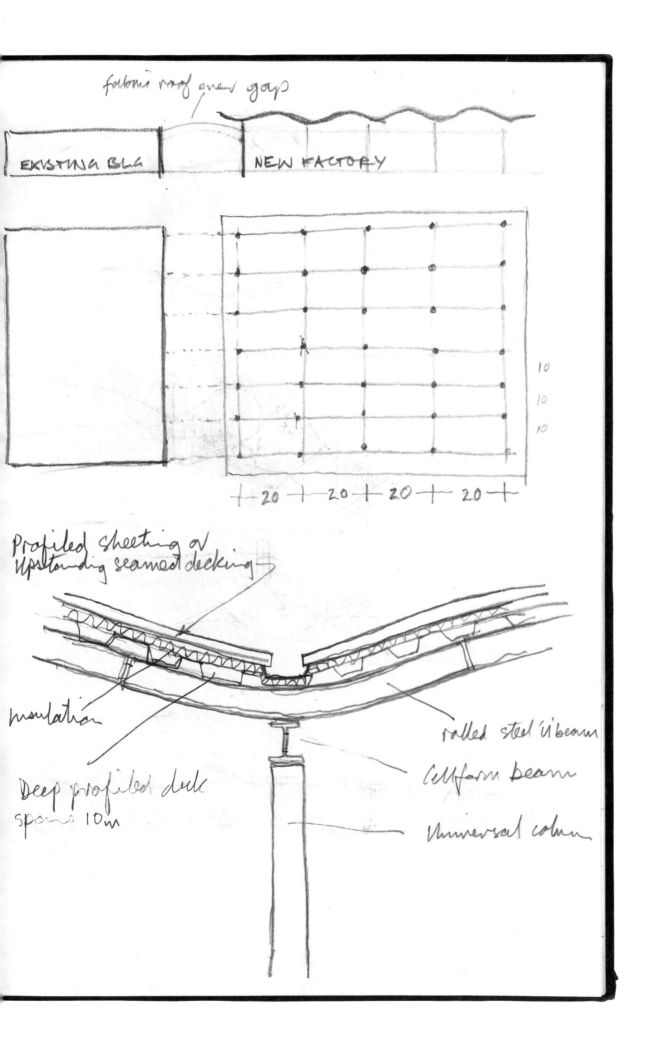

fabric roof over gaps

EXISTING BLG

NEW FACTORY

10
10
10

+ 20 + 20 + 20 + 20 +

Profiled sheeting or
Upstanding seamed decking

insulation

Deep profiled deck
spans 10m

rolled steel 'i'beam

Cellform beam

Universal column

SEINE BRIDGE
Design session   Aug 98

RC bra

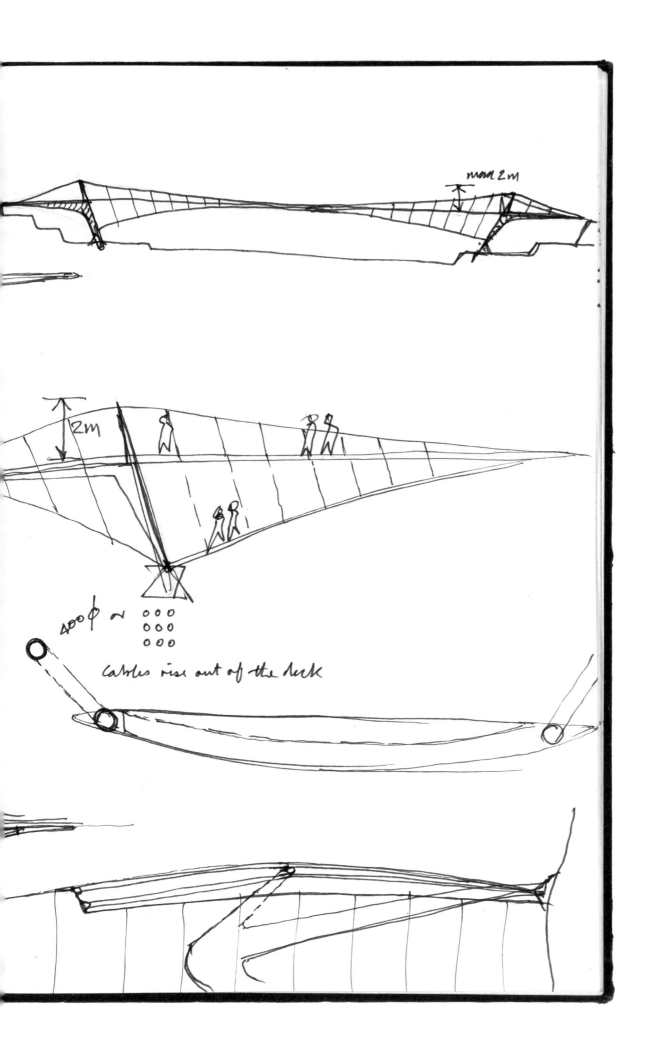

mod 2m

2m

400 ⌀ or ○○○
            ○○○
            ○○○

Cables rise out of the deck

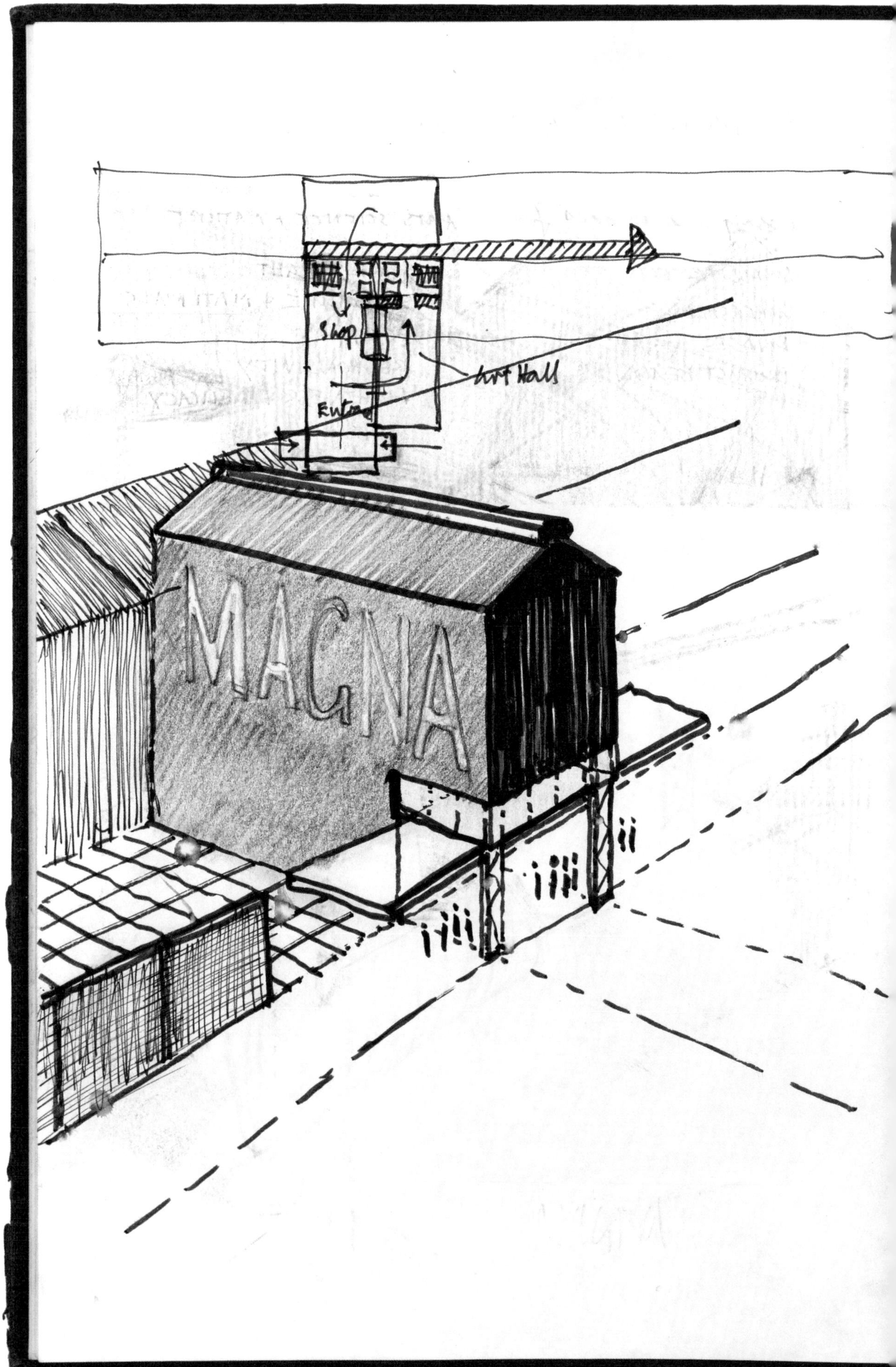
Shop
Art Hall
MAGNA

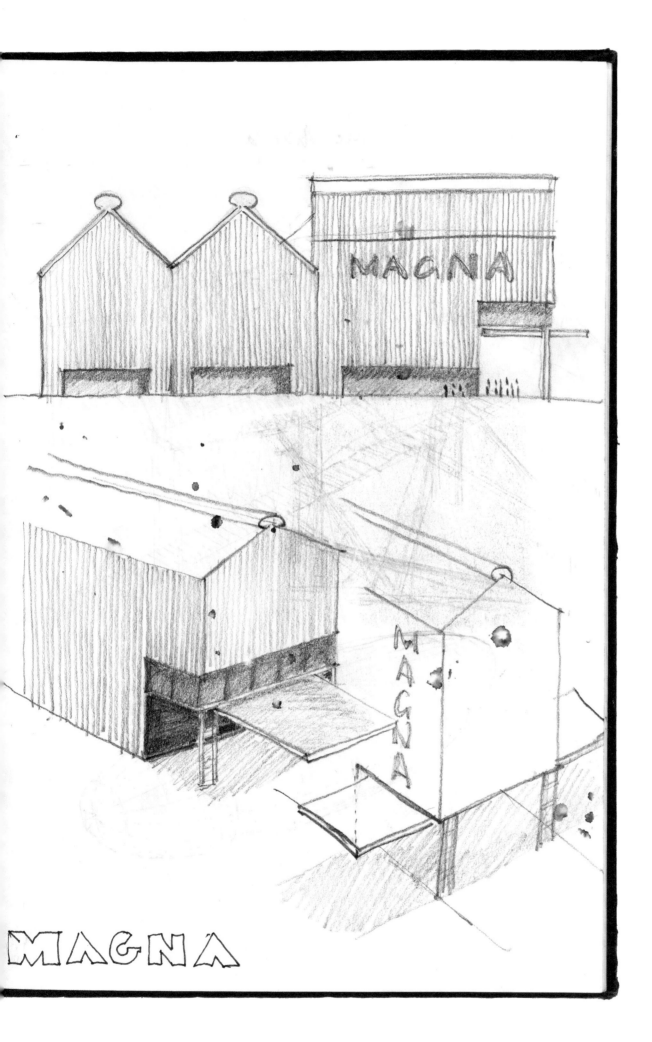

MAGNA

AIR

EGG in fabric like a Dirigible

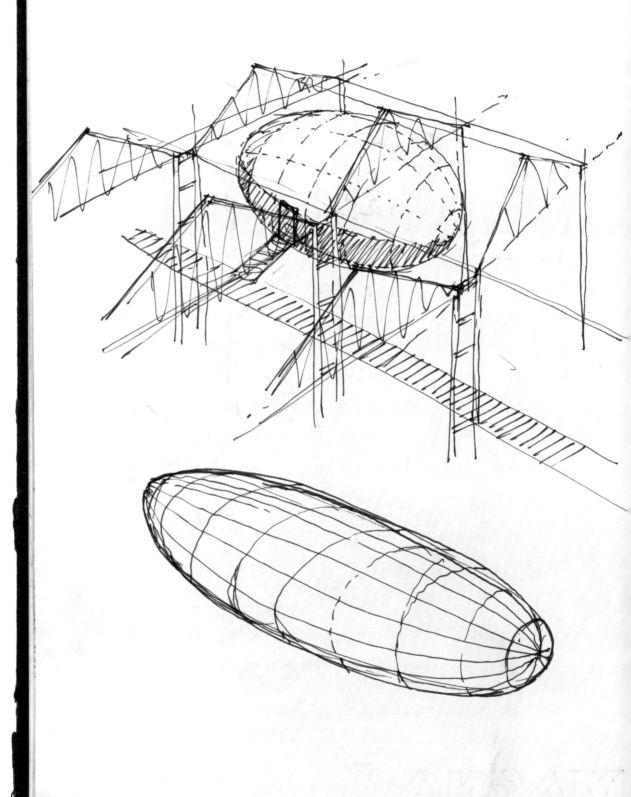

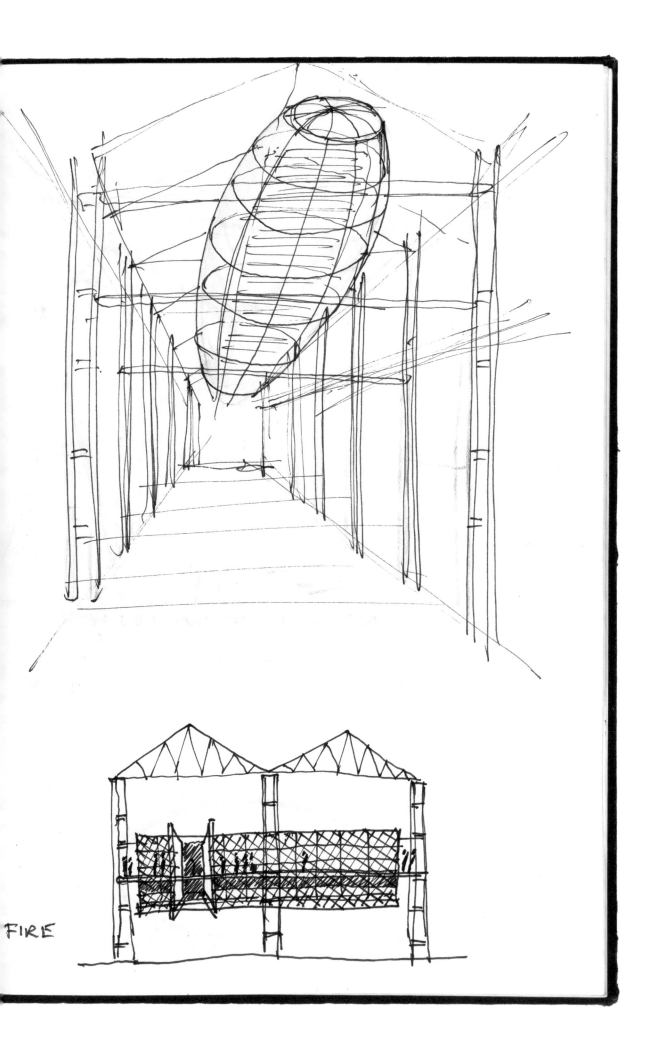

FIRE

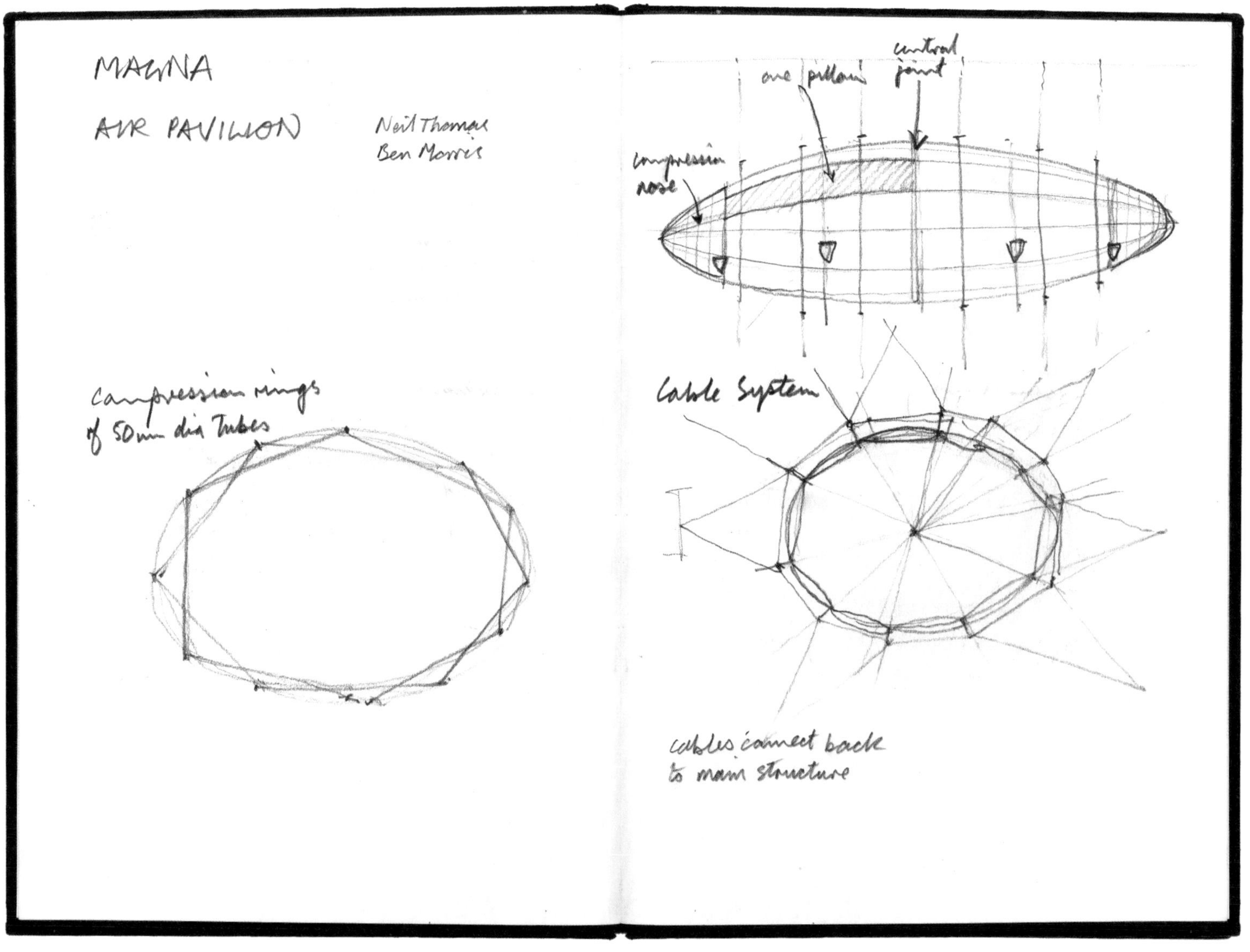

MAGNA

AIR PAVILION   Neil Thomas
                Ben Morris

compression rings
of 50mm dia Tubes

central
joint
one pillar
compression
nose

Cable System

cables connect back
to main structure

WATER PAVILION FOR MAGNA

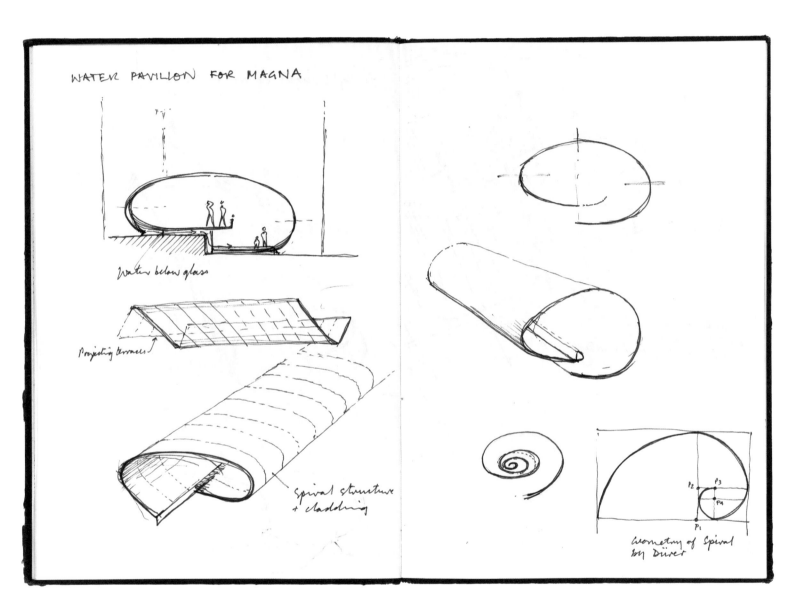

Water below glass

Projecting terraces

Spiral structure
+ cladding

Geometry of Spiral
by Dürer

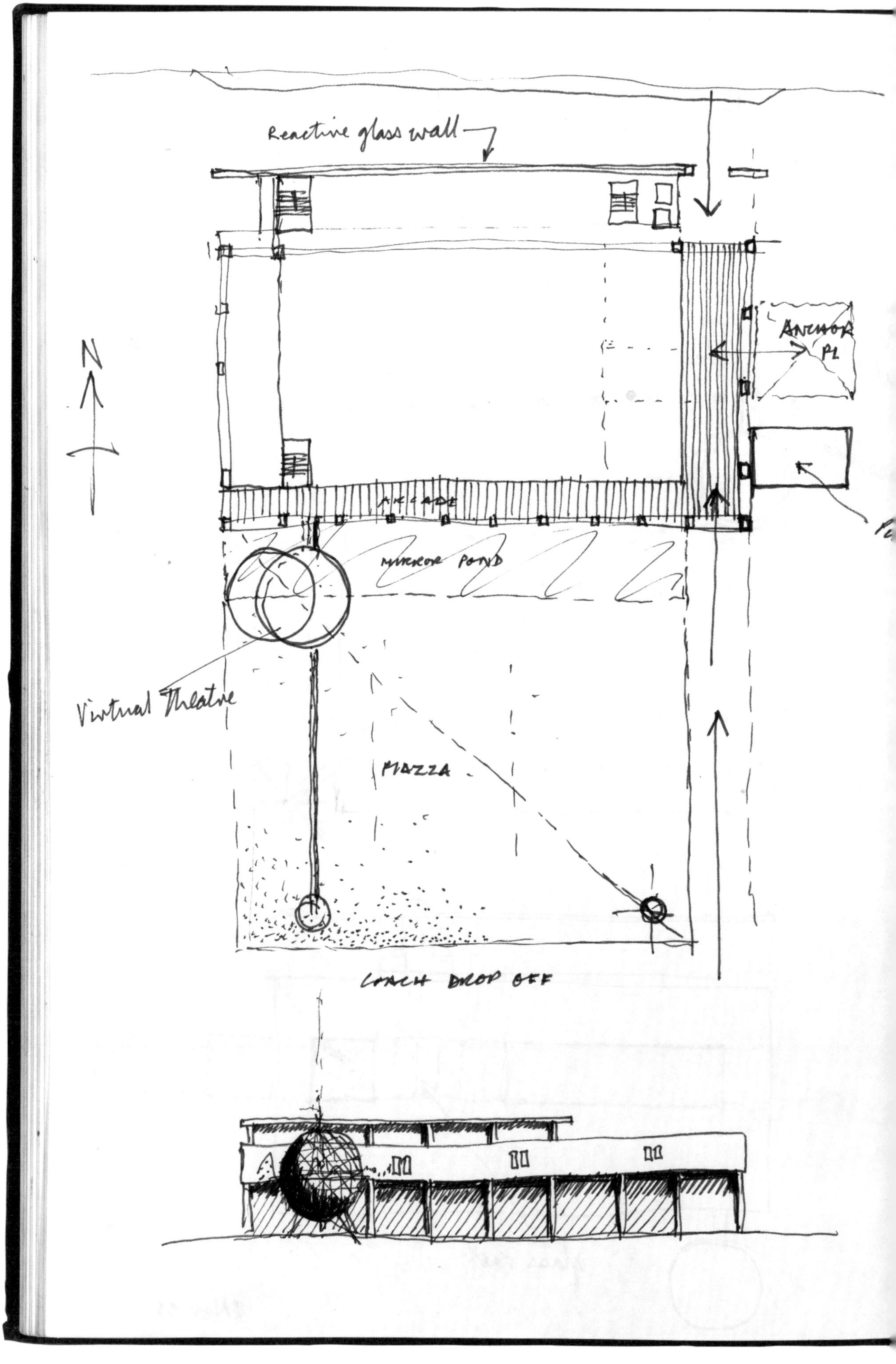

reactive glass wall

N

ANCHOR PL

ARCADE

MIRROR POND

Virtual Theatre

PIAZZA

COACH DROP OFF

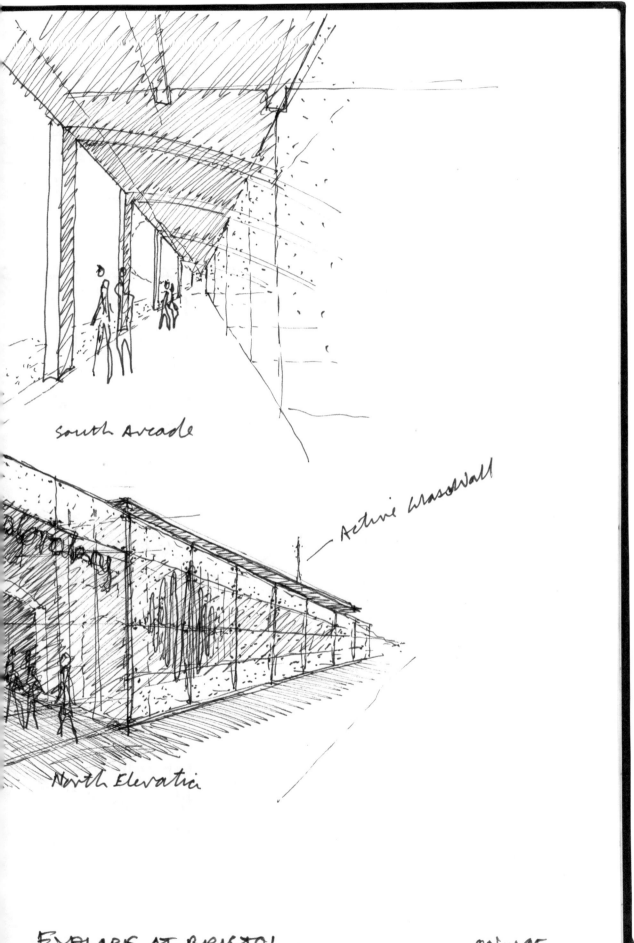

south Arcade

Active GlassWall

North Elevation

EXPLORE AT BRISTOL   8 Nov 95

ARCADE onto New Piazza for Explore @ Bristol

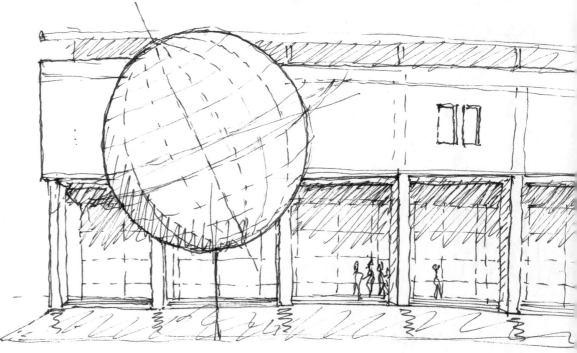

SHOP FRONT onto Road

Active glass wall
fronts on to the ro

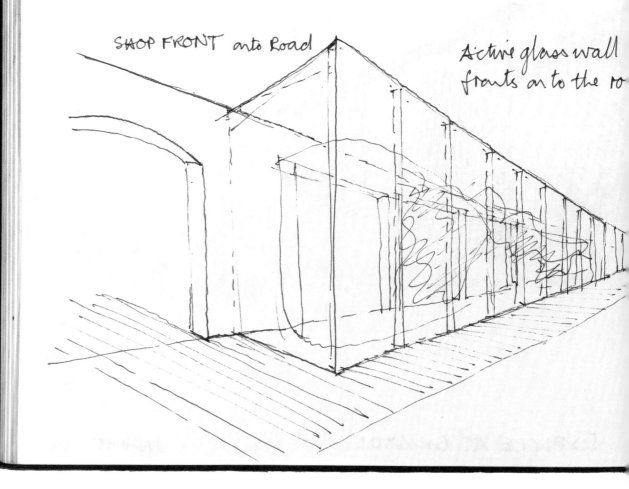

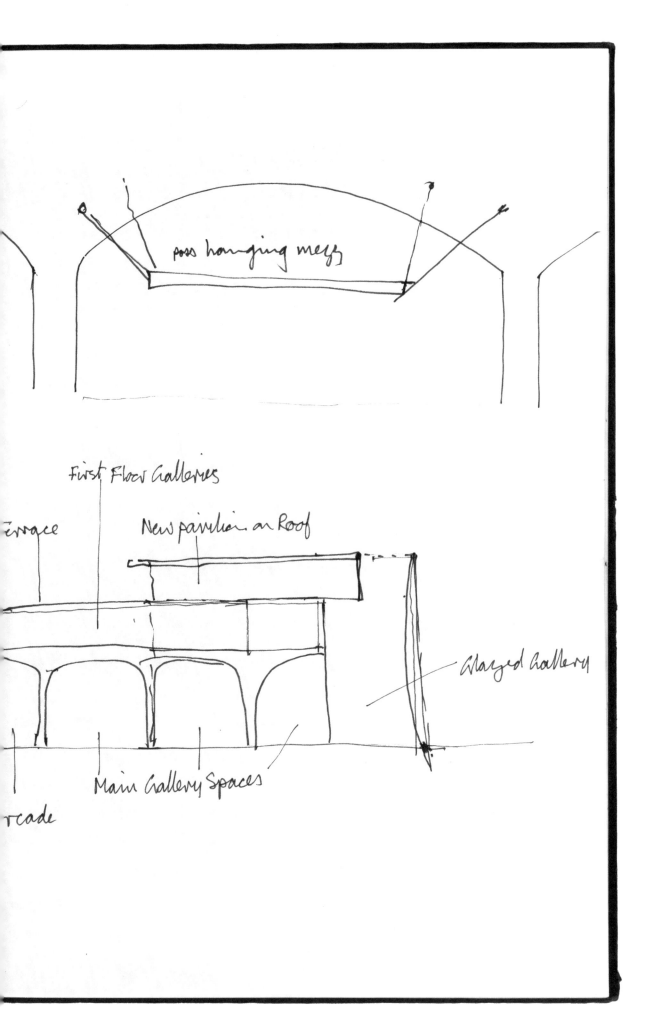

poss hanging mezz

First Floor Galleries

Terrace

New pavilion on Roof

Glazed Gallery

Main Gallery Spaces

rcade

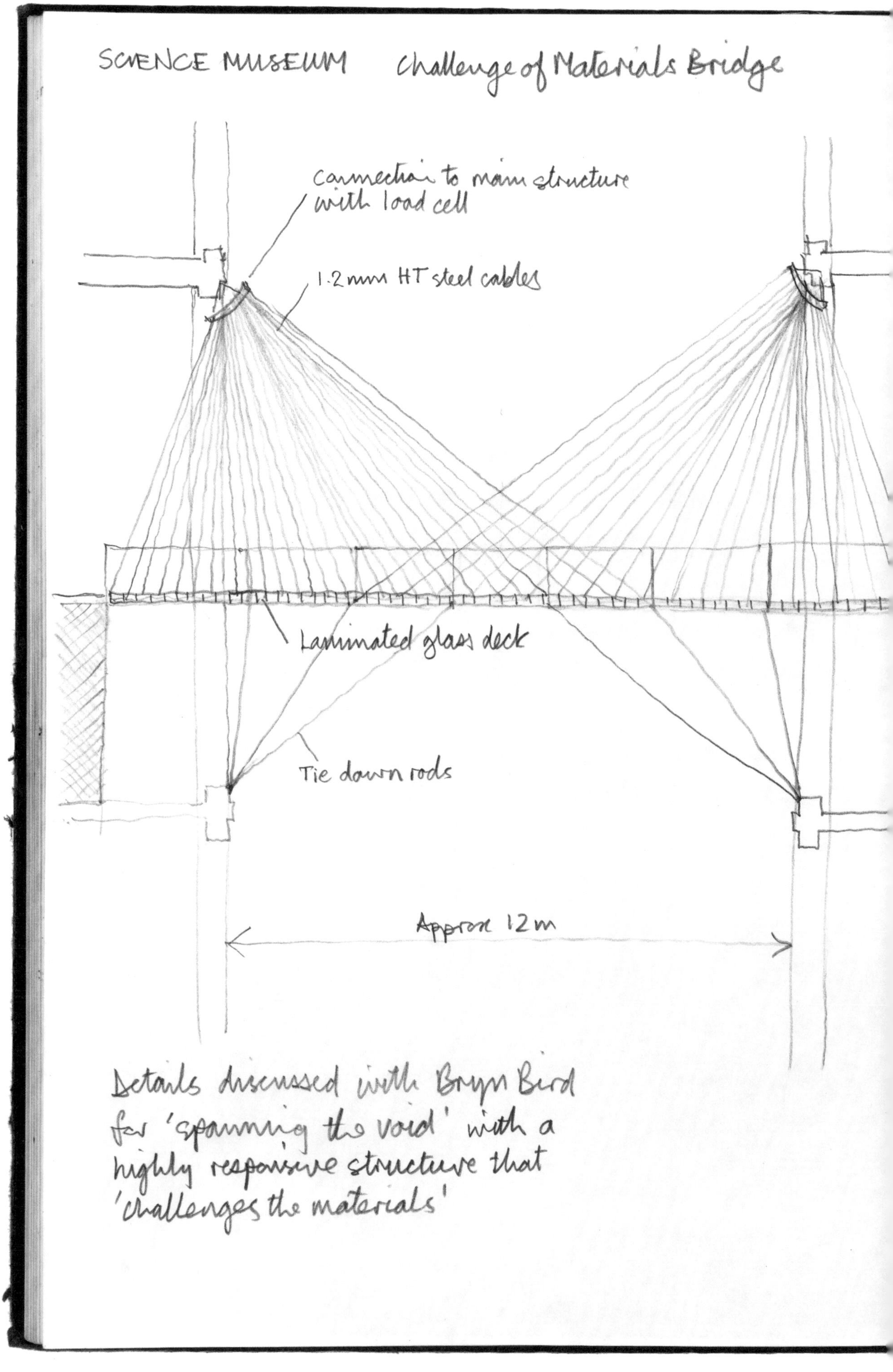
SCIENCE MUSEUM Challenge of Materials Bridge
connection to main structure with load cell
1.2 mm HT steel cables
Laminated glass deck
Tie down rods
Approx 12 m
Details discussed with Bryn Bird for 'spanning the void' with a highly responsive structure that 'challenges the materials'

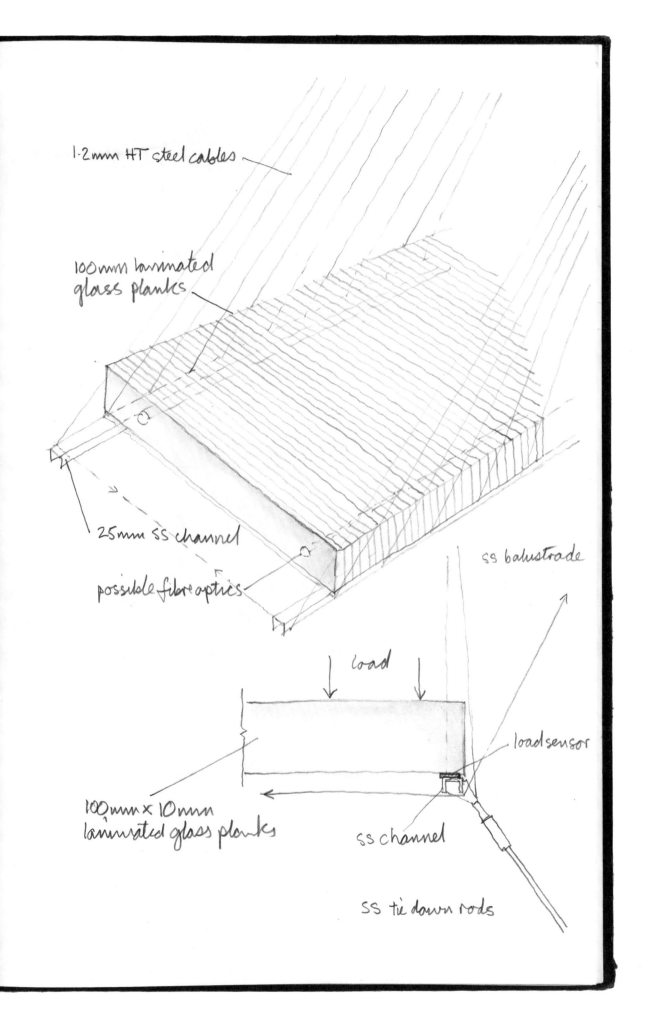

1·2mm HT steel cables

100mm laminated
glass planks

25mm ss channel

possible fibre optics

ss balustrade

load

load sensor

100mm × 10mm
laminated glass planks

ss channel

ss tie down rods

CARPHONE WAREHOUSE   at Merry Hill

an expression of latest technology
with prefabricated pod construction

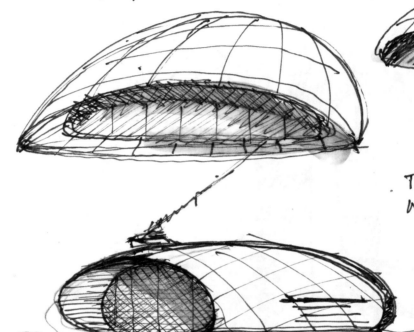

Timber gridshell
with fibreglass pods

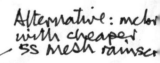

Alternative: melon
with cheaper
SS mesh rainscreen

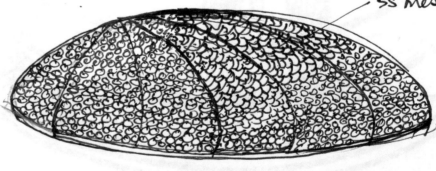

1·4

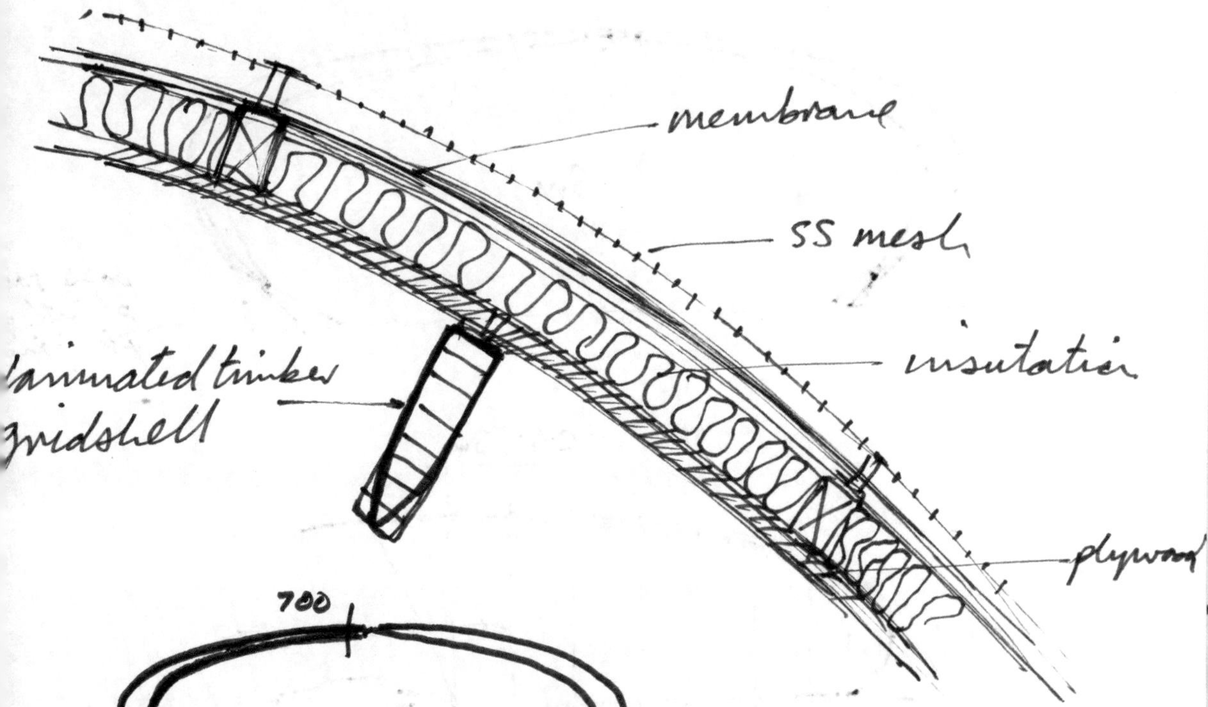

membrane

SS mesh

insulation

laminated timber gridshell

plywood

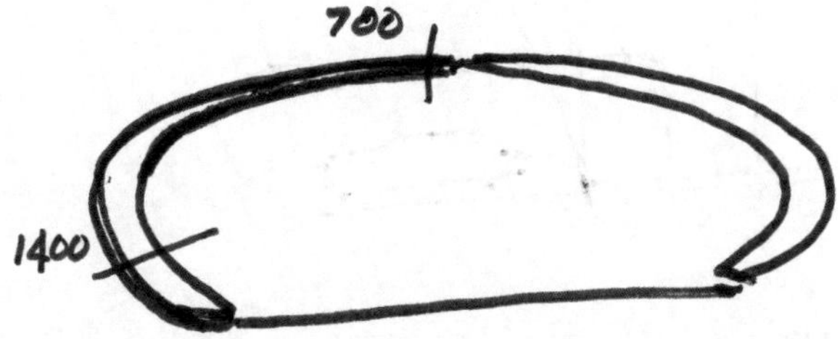

700

1400

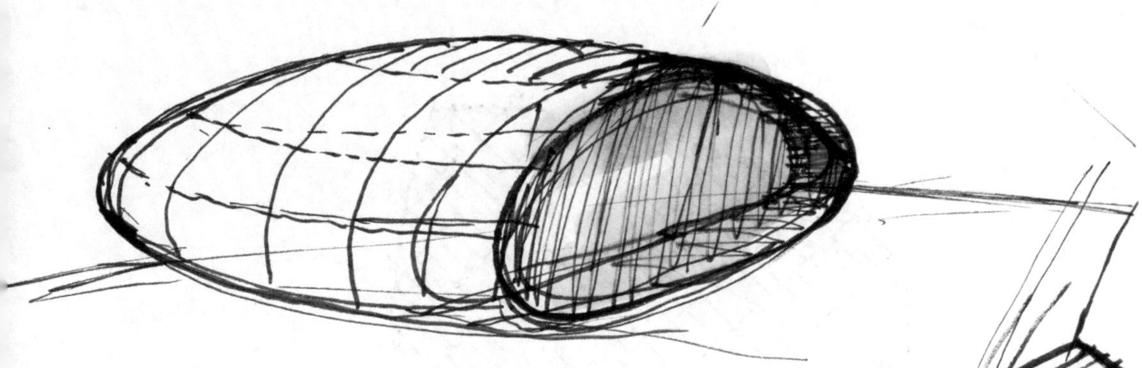

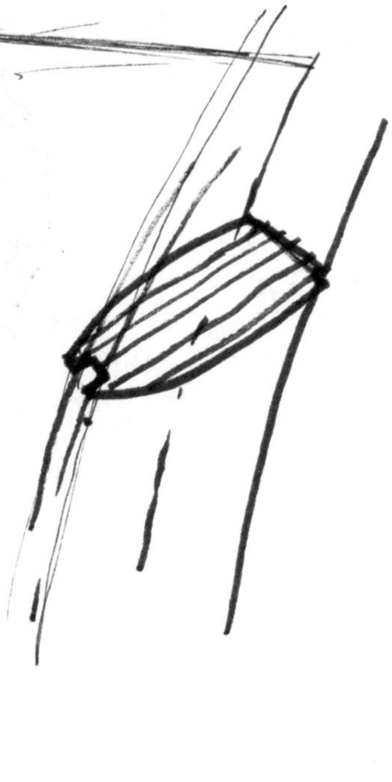

$$\rho \frac{a^2}{x^2} + q \frac{b^2}{y^2} + \frac{rc^2}{z^2} = 0$$

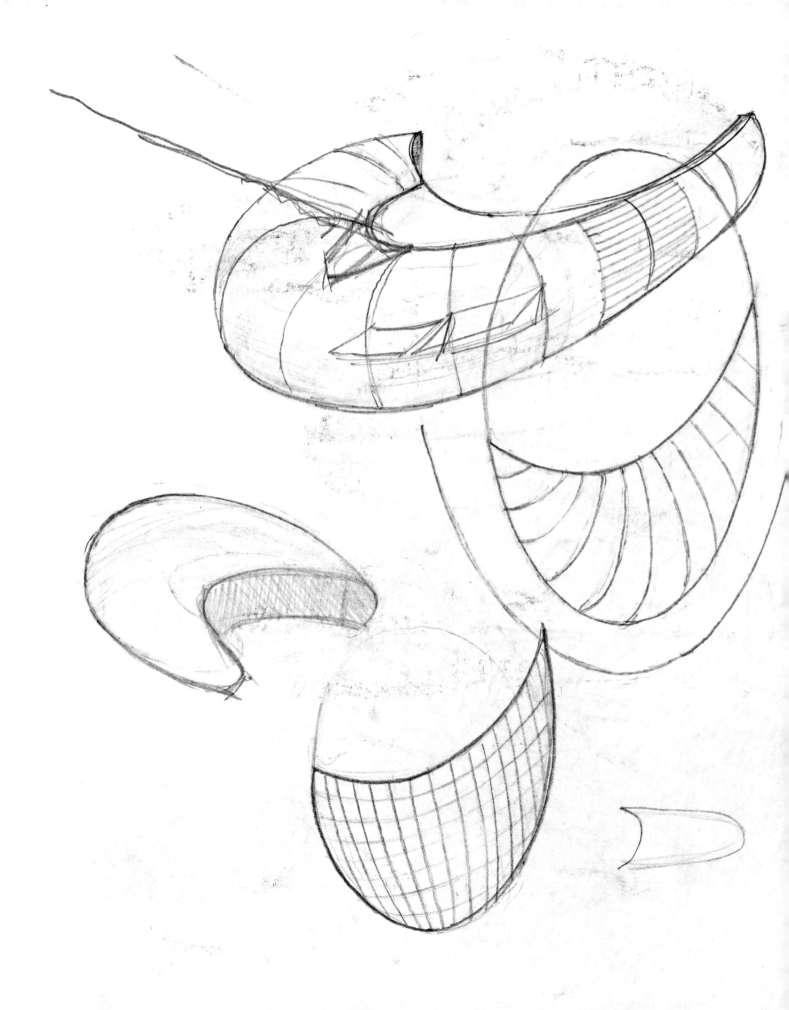

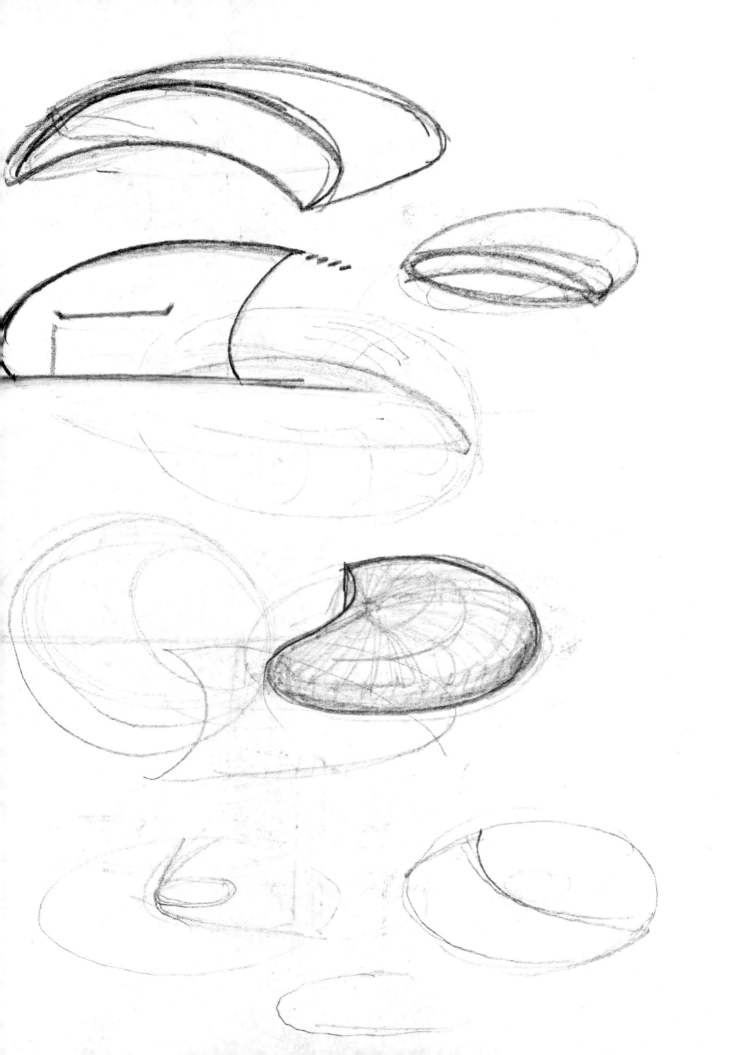

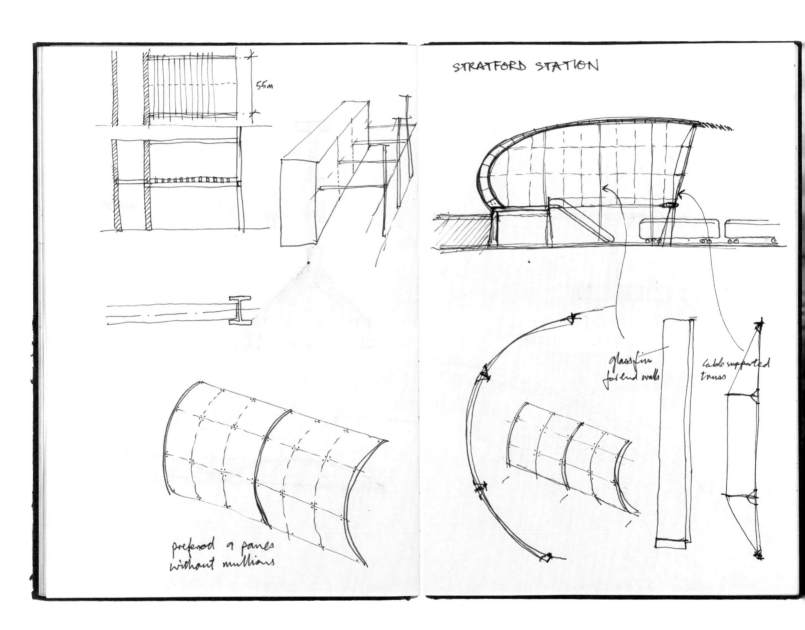

STRATFORD STATION

glass fins
for end walls

cable supported
truss

prefered 9 panes
without mullions

5.5m

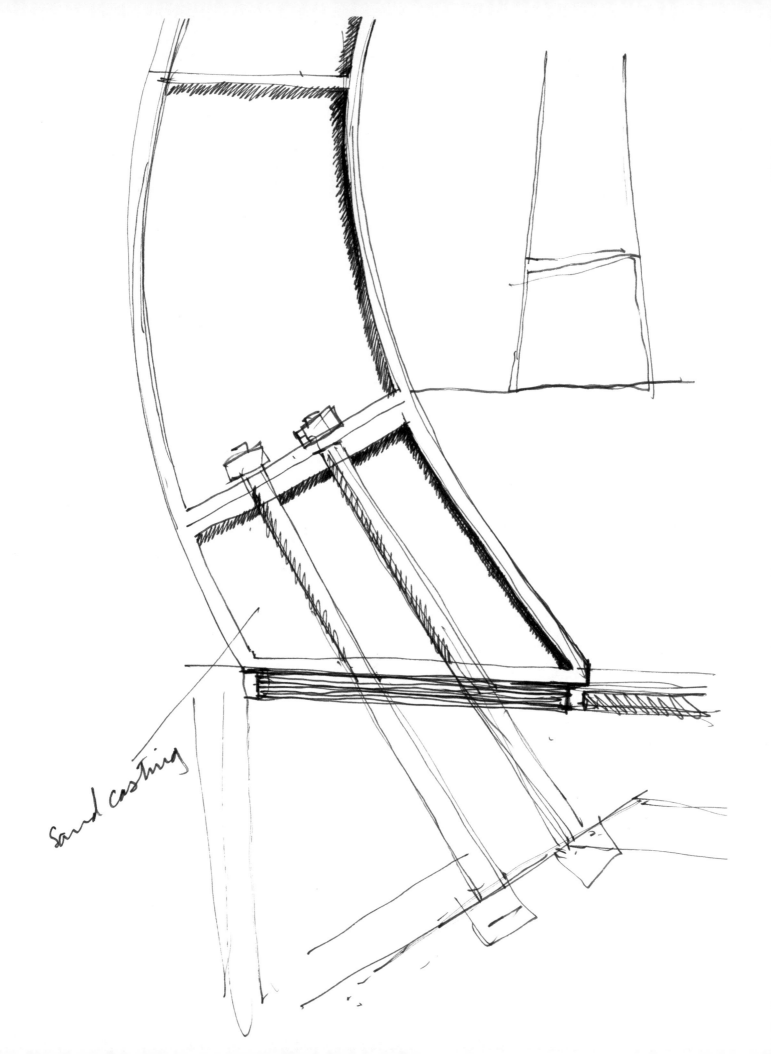

sand casting

STRATFORD MARKET DEPOT   June 91

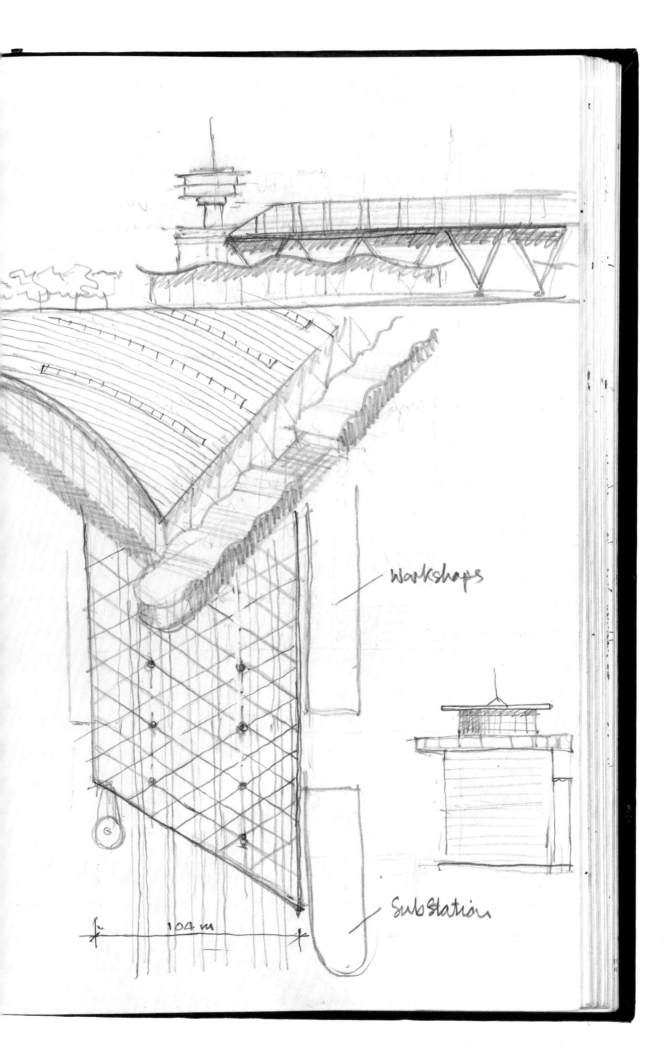

Workshops

Substation

104 m

Pages 10–17
Maggie's Centre | Oxford, UK
Client: Maggie's | Completed 2014

This cancer-caring centre sited on the edge of the Churchill Hospital was designed as a 'tree house'. The sloping site enables access from a bridge, with the building's spaces 'floating' 4 m up in the trees.

The angular geometry was designed to create drama and visual interest to help lift visitors' spirits.

Pages 18–27
Crown Hotel | Sydney, Australia
Client: Crown Hotels | Completion due 2019

The sculptural form of this 70-storey resort hotel in Sydney was modelled on three petals. The faces twist through 70° as they rise to 275 m.

The building will appear in the context of other landmarks on Sydney's Darling Harbour waterfront: the Sydney Harbour Bridge, the Opera House and the tall buildings of the central business district.

The sketches trace the ideas from competition stage through to more detailed design studies.

Pages 28–29
Prussian Blue | London, UK
Client: Mitsubishi Estate London
Completion due 2018

Design for a 40-storey tower in the heart of the City of London on the corner of Leadenhall Street and Bishopsgate. Sketches show the iterative design process that was a fundamental part of meetings with the city planners. Three options were explored, leading to the final scheme of three stacked elements that was submitted for planning in May 2015.

Pages 30–31
Bristol Arena | Bristol, UK
Competition entry 2015

Following an international competition, Wilkinson Eyre was shortlisted to design the 12,000-capacity Bristol Arena.

Pages 32–35
King's Cross Gasholders | London, UK
Client: King's Cross Central Limited Partnership | Completion due 2016

The historic 1850s trio of cast-iron gasholder frames has been renovated and will house two hundred new apartments. The design has a heavy industrial aesthetic on the outside and a more refined 'watchmaker' narrative for the interiors that relates to the three interlocking circular forms. The scheme, which was won in 2005, was put on hold until 2013 and work started on site in 2015.

The sketches show the early competition scheme, followed by the developed design for construction.

Pages 36–37
Dyson Headquarters Remodelling
Malmesbury, UK | Client: Dyson Ltd
Completion due 2016

The sketches show concept ideas for the Research Building at the Dyson headquarters. This is clad entirely in large reflective glass panels that render the building nearly invisible in its rural landscape.

Pages 38–39
Battersea Power Station | London, UK
Client: Battersea Power Station Development
Company | Completion due 2019

In 2013 Wilkinson Eyre was appointed
for the refurbishment of the iconic
Grade-II listed Battersea Power Station.
The proposed designs are consistent
with and sympathetic to Sir Giles Gilbert
Scott's masterpiece: the chimneys and
turbine halls will remain the dominant
features of the building.

This is an early site drawing at
competition stage.

Pages 40–45
Mary Rose Museum | Portsmouth, UK
Client: The Mary Rose Trust
Completed 2013

A new museum to house King
Henry VIII's favourite warship, the
Mary Rose, which sank in 1545 and
was raised in 1982. The ship has been
restored with 1,900 objects discovered
over the past 30 years, creating a time
capsule of the Tudor era.

The architecture was developed from
the inside out with the *Mary Rose* as
the jewel and the form and materials
selected to suit the historic context. The
sketchbooks show the development of
early ideas through to the completed
building in 2013.

Pages 46–47
Splashpoint Leisure Centre | Worthing, UK
Client: Worthing Borough Council
Completed 2013

A competition-winning design for
municipal pools and a leisure centre on
the beachfront at Worthing. The main
pool hall acts as a viewfinder, connecting
Brighton Road with the seafront. The
building terminates in a series of glazed
façades directly overlooking the water.

Pages 52–53
Olympic Velodrome | London, UK
Competition entry 2007

Unsuccessful competition entry for
the London 2012 Olympic Games.
The winning design was presented by
Michael Hopkins Architects.

Pages 48–49
Landscape to Portrait | London, UK
Client: Royal Academy of Arts | Exhibited 2012

Art installation in the Royal Academy's
Annenberg Courtyard for the 2012
Summer Exhibition.

The idea was based on picture frames
set out on a sine curve that twist from
landscape format as you arrive, through
to portrait as you leave. The frames are
set in a polished stainless steel base that
reflects the sky and the buildings around
the courtyard.

These sketches show the early concept
that was presented to the Summer
Exhibition Committee, followed by the
development of the chosen designs.

Pages 50–51
The Crystal | London, UK
Client: Siemens | Completed 2012

First ideas through to design concept
for this urban sustainability centre,
designed for Siemens and completed
to coincide with the London 2012
Olympic Games.

This highly sustainable construction
challenges preconceptions: despite
having a fully glazed exterior, the
building produces all its own energy
and recycles water.

Pages 54–57
Guangzhou International Finance Center
Guangzhou, China | Client: Yuexiu Property
Group | Completed 2011

This design won an international
competition in 2005. One of the tallest
buildings in the world at 440 m,
the center's fully glazed, rounded
triangular form is an elegant addition
to the skyline of China's third city.

The huge diagrid structure, which can
be seen through the glazed façade, gives
lateral stiffness to the tower and provides
a 34-storey atrium for the hotel at the top.

Pages 58–59
Boundary Monument | Gretna, UK
Competition entry 2011

Unsuccessful competition scheme
for a monument at Gretna to mark
the boundary between England and
Scotland.

Pages 60–61
Factory conversion | Bologna, Italy
Competition entry 2015

Unsuccessful competition entry for the
conversion of Pier Luigi Nervi's tobacco
factory in Bologna.

Page 62
Ironmongery
Concept for King's Cross Gasholders

Ideas for bespoke ironmongery for
the King's Cross Gasholders project
(see pp. 32–35).

Page 63
Chaise longue
Personal project

Ideas for a chair upholstered with
a structured material that mimics the
make-up of muscle tissue.

Pages 64–65
University of Exeter: Forum Project
Exeter, UK | Client: University of Exeter
Completed 2012

A timber-grid shell connects the
library with the administration building,
creating social facilities for students.
The modular construction facilitates
an irregular curved form, which is
in tune with the contoured landscape
and is illustrated in these early
concept sketches.

Pages 66–67
University of Sharjah Canopies
Sharjah, United Arab Emirates | Concept, 2009

A project to design a system of canopies
for solar shading at the University
of Sharjah, which was developed to
a detailed stage but unrealised.

Pages 68–69
Media City Footbridge | Salford, UK
Client: Peel Holdings | Completed 2011

Early sketches for a bridge over the
Manchester Ship Canal, now known as
the Media City Footbridge. The bridge
has a span of 90 m and rotates to allow
ships to pass.

Pages 70–73
Arts Two | London, UK | Client: Queen Mary,
University of London | Completed 2011

Early sketches for the Graduate School,
currently under construction, and the
Humanities Department, completed
in 2011, show a commitment to enliven
this university campus off London's
Mile End Road.

Pages 74–75
Arundel Great Court | London, UK
Client: Land Securities
Planning permission granted

Sketches prepared at the public
inquiry to demonstrate that the
glazing proportions of the proposed
new building are in keeping with the
proportions of the nearby church of
St Mary le Strand.

Pages 76–77
Department of Earth Sciences | Oxford, UK
Client: University of Oxford | Completed 2011

Sketches show proposals for the
'narrative wall', which adjoins the
Laboratory Block on South Parks Road.
The concept takes rock strata as its
inspiration, an interpretation rendered
using natural stones on a concrete
base panel.

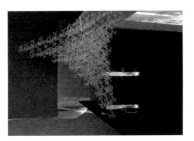

Pages 78–79
'Reflections' Installation | Venice, Italy
Client: Venice Biennale | Exhibited 2004

Design proposal for the Wilkinson
Eyre installation at the 2004 Venice
Biennale, in which images and models
are reflected onto a water table. Sketches
of Venice are also included.

Pages 80–81
Apraksin Dvor Masterplan | St Petersburg,
Russia | Client: Glavstroy Spb | Completed 2009

Competition-winning scheme for a
major urban redevelopment of the
Market District in St Petersburg,
fronting the Fontanka Canal.

Pages 82–83
Jeddah Central District | Jeddah, Saudi Arabia
Concept

Scheme for the regeneration of Jeddah
with an island in the Red Sea that
encloses 1 km² of water. Tidal movement
creates a mechanism by which polluted
water is flushed from the harbour and
inlets of this historic city.

Pages 84–89
Liverpool Arena and Convention Centre
Liverpool, UK | Client: Liverpool City Council
Completed 2008

Two curvilinear forms, connected by
a glazed galleria, enclose a 10,000-seat
arena on one side and an exhibition and
conference centre on the other.

The sketches, which explore structure,
form and materiality, were undertaken
over a two- to three-year design period
for the building, which was completed
in 2008.

Pages 90–91
Audi Regional Headquarters | London, UK
Client: Audi UK | Completed 2009

Competition sketches for the regional headquarters in Glasgow and design concept for the London headquarters at Hammersmith, completed in 2009.

Pages 92–93
Leamouth Bridge
London City Island, UK | Client: Ballymore Properties Ltd | Competition entry 2015

Design proposals for a footbridge at Leamouth across the river to Canning Town station. Unrealised.

Pages 94–95
Amnesty International Pavilion | Milan, Italy
Client: House of Human Rights, in Collaboration with Amnesty International
Concept design 2007

Design sketch for a pavilion in Milan to house Amnesty International and other charities. Presented at the Milan Furniture Fair in 2007.

Pages 96–97
Tate Modern Extension | London, UK
Competition entry 2004

Sketches of ideas presented for invited competition in 2004. Unrealised.

Pages 98–99
Royal Botanic Garden Edinburgh
Edinburgh, UK | Competition entry 2003
Unsuccessful competition entry in 2003.

Pages 100–03
Crystal Palace | London, UK
Client: Crystal Palace Campaign Committee
Concept design 2003

Design proposals for a new arts building on the site of the old Crystal Palace at Sydenham. This was commissioned by the Crystal Palace Campaign Committee but unrealised.

Pages 104–07
National Waterfront Museum | Swansea, UK
Clients: National Museum Wales / City and County of Swansea | Completed 2005

Competition-winning concept ideas for this museum in Swansea.

Pages 108–13
Dyson Headquarters | Malmesbury, UK
Client: Dyson Ltd | Completed 1999

Early concept ideas for the Dyson headquarters date back to 1997, with details for the entrance and the distinctive roofscape.

Pages 114–15
Seine Bridge | Paris, France
Competition entry 1999

Competition design for a footbridge across the River Seine giving access from France's national library to Parc de Bercy. Unrealised.

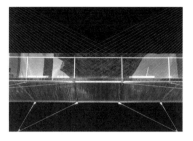

Pages 116–21
Magna Science Adventure Centre
Rotherham, UK | Client: The Magna Trust
Completed 2001

Scheme for the transformation of the redundant Templeborough Steelworks at Rotherham into a science centre with Millennium Commission funding. The project was completed in 2001 and won the Stirling Prize that year. The four pavilions have a narrative of earth, fire, air and water, and are connected by bridges within the enormous steel sheds.

Pages 122–25
Explore@Bristol Science Centre | Bristol, UK
Client: @Bristol | Completed 1999

Competition-winning scheme for transforming a train shed in Bristol into a science centre, with funding from the Millennium Commission.

Pages 126–27
Challenge of Materials Bridge | London, UK
Client: Science Museum | Completed 1997

A glass bridge across the atrium of the Science Museum supported by 1.5-mm diameter high-tensile steel cables, hanging from the existing structure. The bridge is wired with sensors and load cells connected to computers that translate visitors' movement across the bridge into light and sound.

Pages 128–31
Carphone Warehouse | Merry Hill, near Dudley, UK | Client: Chelsfield plc | Concept, 1997

This scheme for a retail warehouse outlet forms a landmark gateway to the main shopping centre. The plan features a double curvature form constructed from laminated plywood. Unrealised.

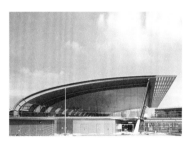

Pages 132–33
Stratford Regional Station | London, UK
Clients: London Underground Ltd / Stratford Development Partnership Ltd / London Borough of Newham | Completed 1999

Sketch details for the Jubilee Line Station project, which was commissioned in 1994 and completed in 1999. Winner of multiple awards.

Pages 134–35
Stratford Depot | London, UK
Client: London Underground Ltd
Completed 1991

Early concept drawings for the Jubilee Line Maintenance Depot at Stratford, which was commissioned in 1991 and completed in 1996. This project provided a turning point for the practice.

Wilkinson Eyre Architects: Works
Emma Keyte and Jay Merrick, London, 2014

Tectonics: A Building for Earth Sciences at Oxford
Stafford Critchlow, Hugh Pearman, Chris Wilkinson et al.,
London, 2011

Bridging Art and Science
Chris Wilkinson and Jim Eyre, London, 2009

Exploring Boundaries: The Architecture of Wilkinson Eyre
Peter Davey and Kurt W. Forster, Basel, 2007

Destinations
Wilkinson Eyre Architects, London, 2005

Bridges
Wilkinson Eyre Architects, London, 2003

Supersheds
Chris Wilkinson, Oxford, 1991

ACKNOWLEDGEMENTS

I am hugely grateful to the Royal Academy for taking on this project. Nick Tite, Peter Sawbridge, Carola Krueger and Kate Goodwin have been supportive, creative and professional during the whole process.

I am so glad that Helen Eger has designed the book with such skill and enthusiasm. She has worked closely with me and the whole team to produce a beautiful and well-coordinated layout. She has been backed up by Michelle Lewis, Rita Vekaria and Violet Bennell at Wilkinson Eyre who have dedicated much time and effort to making it happen. I couldn't have done this without the amazing support of Linda Lenthall in the office and Diana Wilkinson at home.

I am indebted to Charles Saumarez Smith for writing such an appropriate introduction and to John Bodkin for photographing my sketchbooks in such a sensitive way.

Chris Wilkinson
July 2015

WilkinsonEyre

First published on the occasion
of the exhibition:
'Thinking Through Drawing:
Chris Wilkinson RA'
Royal Academy of Arts, London
3 September 2015 – 14 February 2016

ROYAL ACADEMY PUBLICATIONS
Beatrice Gullström
Alison Hissey
Carola Krueger
Simon Murphy
Peter Sawbridge
Nick Tite

Picture research: Wilkinson Eyre
Sketchbook photography:
John Bodkin, DawkinsColour, London
Design: Studio Eger
Colour origination:
DawkinsColour, London
Printed in Florence
by Conti Tipocolor

British Library Cataloguing-in-
Publication Data
A catalogue record for this book is
available from the British Library

ISBN 978-1-910350-18-8

Distributed outside the United States
and Canada by Thames & Hudson
Ltd, London

Distributed in the United States and
Canada by Harry N. Abrams, Inc.,
New York

ILLUSTRATIONS

Page 1: Chris Wilkinson's
sketchbooks
Page 2: Concept sketch for King's
Cross Gasholders, London, UK
Page 4: Concept sketches for
Portrait to Landscape, the Annenberg
Courtyard installation at the Royal
Academy Summer Exhibition 2012

PHOTOGRAPHIC ACKNOWLEDGEMENTS

All photographs in 'Drawing
What I Think', pp. 6–9, and
'Key to Illustrated Projects',
pp. 136–43 are © Wilkinson
Eyre Architects, excluding:

Page 138: Kings Cross © V1 |
Page 139: Mary Rose Museum
and Splashpoint Leisure Centre
© Julian Abrams | Page 141: Queen
Mary, University of London © Morley
von Sternberg | Page 142: Audi
Regional HQ © Leon Chew; National
Waterfront Museum © James
Brittain; Dyson HQ © Timothy Soar
| Page 143: Magna © Edmund
Sumner / VIEW; Explore © Susan
Kay; Challenge of Materials Bridge
© James Morris; Stratford Regional
Station © Dennis Gilbert; Stratford
Market Depot © JLEP.